FROM PAGE TO STAGE

From Page To Stage

Selecting and Adapting Literature
for Readers Theatre by

Marvin Kaye

With a Preface by

Judy E. Yordon

With Four Award-winning Scripts by

Constance Alexander
Ted Eiland
Steve Schaeffer
Robert Hawkins

Garden City, New York

The support, encouragement and assistance of the following persons made this volume possible: special thanks to Professor Louis Fantasia; Beth Goehring, editor of *The Fireside Theatre;* Charles LaBorde; Morgan Llywelyn; Mary Stuart; Nancy Temple, charter member and publicity director of The Open Book; George White, founder and president of the Eugene O'Neill National Theater Center, and Professor Judy E. Yordon.

Design by Maria Chiarino
Manufactured in the U.S.A.
ISBN: 1-56865-176-7

Contents

Preface

What is Readers Theatre?

As the winning scripts attest in this edition, readers theatre is a flexible, creative medium for presenting all kinds of literary texts.

Earliest Readers Theatre Production

The term "readers theatre" was probably used for the first time in 1945 in New York, when *Oedipus Rex* was produced by a professional group who called themselves Readers Theatre, Inc. Their stated purpose was "to give the people of New York an opportunity to witness performances of great dramatic works which were seldom if ever produced." Performance groups like The Open Book allow this great tradition to continue.

Readers Theatre Text Material

As the scripts in this volume indicate, traditional readers theatre works best with texts that make their primary appeal to our auditory sense. Texts which feature evocative images, for example, can benefit from readers theatre staging which features economy and suggestion (not literalizing elements, in order to promote audience participation). Readers theatre depends on synecdochical spectacle—using a part to suggest the whole. The Royal Shakespeare Company's recent staging of Homer's poem "The Odyssey," for example, calls for someone to portray a one-eyed monster, the Cyclops, to transform Odysseus' men into pigs and to suggest a ship at sea. As Richard Corliss, reviewing "The Odyssey" for *Time Magazine*, wrote, "The Odyssey" puts "epic dreams on a bare stage, to evoke ancient empires with only words and a few props." Material that might be effectively staged in readers theatre appeals to the audience's imagination. Audiences benefit from being able to experience literature which does not normally get staged.

In recent years, the popularity of readers theatre has grown tremendously, although rarely are "readers theatre" productions called "readers theatre." They are simply accepted as "theatre" productions and audiences may not be aware that they are often witnessing material not originally intended for the stage. Some shows, like *Cats*, adapted from T. S. Eliot's collection of poems, *Old Possum's Book of Practical Cats*, run for years on Broadway. Productions of such novels as *The Grapes of Wrath*, *The Scarlet Letter*, *Jane Eyre*, *Nicholas Nickleby*, *Great Expectations*, *As I Lay Dying*, *A Clockwork Orange*, *The Secret Garden*, *Les Miserables* and so on, are testimonials to the success of transforming nondramatic texts for the stage. In addition, many play texts can be presentationally staged in a readers theatre format. A. R. Gurney's *Love Letters*, for example, is a two-person play which is essentially a readers theatre compilation of letters exchanged between two fictitious characters. Other plays which can effectively be staged in readers theatre style include *Equus*, *Our Town*, *The Elephant Man*, *Agnes of God*, *Amadeus*, and Dylan Thomas' radio play *Under Milk Wood*.

Readers Theatre Conventions

As stated before, the earliest readers theatre productions made almost no use of sets, lights, costumes, make-up, etc., or physical movement. Readers—attired in white shirts/blouses and dark pants/skirts—usually sat on stools behind music stands or lecterns and read from manuscripts. There were no literal exits or entrances; the cast remained onstage throughout the performance, looking up or down, turning forward or back, standing or sitting to suggest coming onto or leaving the playing area. Readers often "read" more than one role, and there may have been unison or choral speaking. These productions were primarily aural and the performers depended on the audience's ability to imagine the visual aspects of the script.

Readers Theatre Today
We have experimented much since those early productions. Readers theatre practitioners now believe that there must be conflict, interaction and some visual appeal for present-day theatre audiences. Many productions now successfully employ staging, spectacle and special effects to underscore the particular material being performed. Stools, music stands and manuscripts are often discarded unless their use is necessary.

Today's readers theatre productions pose a dual responsibility on directors. They must make sure that the readers keep the text as the featured element of the production. They must, however, make sure to keep the *theatre* in readers theatre—that "theatrical complement" which pays attention to the needs most audience members have for visual stimulation, including physical movement and minimal spectacle elements. Not that we want readers theatre to lose its special appeal to the audience's imagination, but we want also to involve the audience's other senses as well. The more involved the audience feels, the more they will appreciate and remember what they have experienced.

Types of Readers Theatre Scripts
As the selections in this text indicate, readers theatre covers a wide range of scripting possibilities, including single texts, expanded program compiled scripts (which deal with several selections on the same theme or idea with transitions between selections), and collage compiled scripts (various selections on the same theme or idea with no transitions between selections so that scripts move seamlessly from one source to the next).

Constance Alexander's winning script, **Kilroy Was Here,**

is a collage text surrounding our entrance into World War II. It includes personal reminiscences along with historical material (e.g., Roosevelt's declaration of war speech), period commercials (e.g., Philip Morris, Kelvinator) and recipes (e.g., meatless sausage patties).

The Most Dangerous Woman by Ted Eiland, co-winner, is a one-woman play which, like **Kilroy Was Here,** is a collage script depicting the activities of Mother Mary Jones— "the first woman union organizer in the United States." Whereas *Kilroy* investigates a personal response to a period in time, *The Most Dangerous Woman* creates a biographical portrait of one particular woman in a dramatic monologue-like format. This script includes historical material from Douglas Baer, National Chairman of the Coal Mine Operators Association, before a congressional commission; direct quotes from General John Chase, head of the state militia in Trinidad; Whitey Gossett, president of the copper miners union; and Lonnie Bostock, the business agent for the textile workers union, among others.

Journeys by Steve Schaeffer is a single-text script on the theme of domestic violence which features the simultaneous reflections of three women. Although the women seem quite different from each other initially, by the end of the script, they share a bond of sisterhood.

The End of a Line by Bob Hawkins is a one-act play for three characters: sisters Nora Ashton and Margaret Gravlee, and a visitor, Mason Miller. This script most resembles a conventional play in that it has defined characters in a defined space, speaking dialogue to each other with no open cognizance of the audience.

Expanding the Dimensions of Readers Theatre
In addition to the conventions of readers theatre staging undergoing some changes, the material readers theatre chooses to stage has evolved. The definitions of both "text" and "per-

formance" have expanded to include non-literary materials and everyday life events. As Richard Schechner, author of *Between Theatre & Anthropology,* attests, "If 'everyday life' is theatre, then people doing ordinary things are performers." There is much in life that is theatrical. Performance is involved in our daily lives since we "play roles" all the time—deciding how to speak in a given circumstance based on "audience," wearing appropriate attire based on occasion, behaving in a certain way because of where we are and what is expected. Life is a kind of lived performance. Personal narratives, stories of all kinds, are possible texts for performance. Aesthetic objects may be considered texts, as well. A quilt may be viewed as a text of a particular family, time period, culture. Rituals may be viewed as social or cultural texts. Demonstrations, rallies and sit-ins may be viewed as political texts. Studies of organizations or diverse cultural groups provide exciting material for group performance texts. Everyday life experiences and conversations may be performed as dialogic texts. Text, then, is a metaphor for all kinds of experiences.

Performance, too, has altered in meaning. Performance is a reflection of humanness, of culture, of communication; performance is a way of knowing. There is theatricality in events and experiences that we may never have considered theatrical. These performance vehicles allow both performers and audiences to learn valuable information about themselves as well as about other people—how they think, operate, talk, interact—information that allows them to taste someone else's reality. Experience with these types of scripts stretches our creativity, makes us more compassionate and prepares us to perform a variety of different kinds of "characters."

Ethnography and Conversation Analysis

Two potential areas for readers theatre scripts are ethnography (the study of cultural groups) and conversation analysis (the study of everyday discourse).

With ethnographic and conversation analysis scripts, we deal with a detailed observation of an everyday life "performance," transcribe this into script form, then translate this script into a new performance experience. Whereas with readers theatre, performers normally enact fictitious characters, in ethnographic and conversation analysis scripts, one attempts to suggest the presence of real people. Whereas with readers theatre, you work from text to performance, with ethnography and conversation analysis, you work from recorded performance to script to re[performance].

These expanded notions of text and performance have rejuvenated readers theatre and allowed for creative growth.

I applaud *The Fireside Theatre* and The Open Book for giving creative writers a chance for healthy experimentation, publication and production.

—*Dr. Judy E. Yordon*
1995, Muncie, Indiana

Introduction

In 1975, a group of professional actors, writers, educators and singers including Bill Bonham, Beverly Fite, Parke Godwin, Saralee Kaye, June Miller, Toby Sanders, Nancy Temple and I began The Open Book, New York City's first professional readers theatre ensemble.

Our purpose was and is to present a wide variety of excellent literature unlikely to be produced by the traditional theatre establishment in a format that deemphasizes modern theatre's scenic elements in order to focus intensively on the artistic experience embodied in the writer's text.

The Open Book's twenty years of slow but steady growth accelerated in 1990 when the company moved to the Amsterdam Room, a nontraditional performing space on Manhattan's West Side at 171 West 85th Street where we specialize in a brand of intimate theatre that in six seasons has included such varied fare as the American premiere of Gerald Moon's *(Corpse)* and Marianne McNaghten's tragedy, *Dearest Nicky, Darling Alex;* the Plautus farce *Assinine;* an *a cappella* musical version of Daniel Pinkwater's popular children's book, *The Hoboken Chicken Emergency,* and the four winners of our first national readers theatre playwrighting competition in 1993.

The success of our play competition, jointly sponsored with *The Fireside Theatre,* has exceeded our initial expectations. We received three hundred and sixty-eight requests for guidelines and ninety-five scripts in 1993. In 1994, for the second competition, we received four hundred and four requests and one hundred and fifty-eight plays, including those in this volume.

We were delighted to receive several new pieces from two of the winners of the first competition, Robert Hawkins of St. Augustine, Florida, and Caroline E. Wood of East Longview,

Washington. Three of their scripts again made it to the finalist stage: Hawkins's **The End of a Line,** included in this
volume, and two others described in Appendix II.

The Open Book originally only intended to produce the
winning entry of the first competition, but we were so over-
whelmed by the quantity and quality of excellent new material suitable for our intimate performing style that we
changed our policy and devoted most of last season to staging
the winner and five other finalist entries, and are producing
all the plays in this volume during 1995 and 1996. As a
testament to the quality of the submissions, two plays tied for
first place: Ted Eiland's powerful one-woman show, **The
Most Dangerous Woman,** and Constance Alexander's evocative "spoken opera," **Kilroy Was Here.**

My thanks to the distinguished panel of judges who selected these winning scripts:

- Beth Goehring, editor of *The Fireside Theatre*
- Charles LaBorde, Charlotte, North Carolina, educator
  and author of the winning script of our first competition,
  Memorial *A Theatrical History of Americans in Viet
  Nam*
- Professor Louis Fantasia, renowned theatrical pro-
  ducer-director-educator, of Los Angeles
- Morgan Llywelyn, best-selling novelist, of Dublin, Ire-
  land
- Mary Stuart, actor-author-singer and star of TV's classic
  Search for Tomorrow, of New York
- Professor Judy E. Yordon, author, educator and readers
  theatre authority, of Ball State University, Muncie, In-
  diana

—Marvin Kaye
Artistic Director
The Open Book, New York City
September 1995

What is Readers Theatre?

Readers theatre is an alternative performance style that draws on both traditional theatrical method and techniques defined and developed at Northwestern University and at various other American college speech departments such as Southern Illinois University, Murray (KY) State College and Pennsylvania State University, which was alma mater to five of the members and one sponsor of The Open Book.

It is a creative, fluid art form capable of presenting all kinds of literature: prose, poetry, drama, even nonfiction in a way calculated to actively involve the audience's imagination in the experience implicit in the writer's text. Strategically, this means three things:

1. Readers theatre is presentational. Sometimes direct audience involvement is minimal; more often it is boldly associative, with verbal forewords, footnotes, asides, soliloquies and direct eye contact with members of the audience. "In this show," I often tell new cast members at The Open Book, "there is no fourth wall . . . or if there is, it's only waist-high. You've got to peek over it now and then." One performer may assume multiple roles, two or more may play one character. Settings, costumes and lighting are minimal, to be fleshed out in the minds of the spectators. Bill Bonham, The Open Book's cofounder and president, says, "It is often referred to as 'theatre of the mind.' " A member of our audience once called it "visual radio." This comparative simplicity of staging sometimes causes theatre people to confuse readers theatre with "staged readings." Unlike staged readings, readers theatre is not a way station in the development of a new play, but an alternative performance style, complete unto itself.

FROM PAGE TO STAGE

2. To many actors, textual illumination only means the motivational study of "beats" and "actions" associated with Stanislavski's method of physical objectives, but in readers theatre, texts must be analyzed, adapted and orchestrated with the meticulous detail that members of a string quartet bring to every measure and note of the music they plan to interpret. The weight, sonority and range of the human voice is applied to the author's denotations, gradations and connotations in order to stir up in the audience's consciousness a verbal (and sometimes literal) music of meaning and emotion that can be far more potent than moods cast by gel-covered lekos on painted flats. At The Open Book, actors learn to speak in unison, chorally, at different rhythms and dynamic levels, fading in and out without losing their places in the text. A direction I frequently employ at the start of a rehearsal period is, "Imagine you are one actor with six heads."

3. Illuminating the experience embodied in the author's text demands selflessness and aesthetic, scholarly sensitivity. Readers theatre is no place for the *auteur*-director.

Readers theatre shares a common heritage with traditional theatre. In an article in the June 1932 issue of the *Quarterly Journal of Speech*, Eugene Bahn traces the beginnings of interpretive reading, from which readers theatre derives, to that moment in the early Greek drama when Thespis stepped forward from the chorus to tell the audience a narrative myth. This is the identical moment that theatre scholars point to when asked to pinpoint the origin of the modern stage.

This common seed suggests that readers theatre is not a new art form, but an old one which speech and oral interpretation professors have rescued and refurbished. The Open Book and The Fireside Theatre are committed to promulgating its viability as a pyrotechnic, yet relatively economical art form.

Staging Readers Theatre

Readers theatre employs a distinctive set of interpretive tools to foreshorten the empathetic distance between the script and the audience. Elaborate scenery, lighting, costuming and other special effects are minimized in favor of elements of presentationalism and sophisticated textual analysis and interpretation.

Casting

Readers theatre interpreters must have flexible, versatile voices and be comfortable speaking directly with the audience. Forming a skillful readers theatre ensemble is artistically demanding and time-consuming, and producers rarely have the option to do so. The ideal solution is to hire performers experienced in readers theatre and oral interpretation techniques. Also actors with cabaret experience, as well as improvisational comics (especially those who work with Keith Johnstone's textbook, *Impro*) tend to adapt well to readers theatre. This is also true of some performers trained in Shakespeare and Molière, presumably because of the presentationalism required by those playwrights.

At The Open Book auditions, I put considerable weight on an actor's ability to "cold read" difficult literature. The second quality I look for is "personal proof," the quality a performer projects upon her or his first entrance. Because readers theatre performers are required to interact with the audience, each actor must be sincere and personable.

Readers theatre is well suited to doubling and countercasting, but neither should be adopted solely to save money. The governing principle should be, how many performers, and of what sort, does the script require to satisfactorily interpret the writer's aesthetic intentions?

Presentationalism

The extent and variety of audience interaction will vary from show to show, but some degree of presentationalism is always present in readers theatre. This is because one of the main goals is to involve the spectators in a shared literary experience. Thus, each performer appears as *a formalized version of her- or himself, acting as intermediary between the literature and the audience.* The duty of the first cast members to appear at the beginning of a show is to establish personal proof, greeting the audience with the distinct subtext, "We have a wonderful literary work to share with you." This goal and context only functions properly when the audience participates (to some extent, both actively and passively) in the cast's work of bringing the author's imagery to life.

One of the director's most important tasks when evaluating a work for readers theatre presentation is to assess its presentational opportunities. Every traditional presentational device is employable: asides and/or soliloquies; use of a narrator, narrators or "Greek chorus"; scenes of action outside the proscenium arch (if there is one); use of the theatre as the actual location of the drama; direct interaction with the audience, either circumscribed, as in Rupert Holmes's *Drood*, which provides alternative text for all possible audience responses, or improvisationally, as in certain kinds of performance art.

In addition to the above techniques, readers theatre performers fulfill any or all of the following presentational tasks:

1. *Introductory:* At the opening of many readers theatre shows, a performer or performers appear in the aforementioned "formalized version of themselves," to introduce the literature, in order to set the mood and/or provide a mental framework for the audience to appreciate what follows. For

example, in The Open Book's recent production of *American Time Capsules*, which included Constance Alexander's **Kilroy Was Here,** the introducer assured the audience that he'd lived through World War II and could vouch for the accuracy of the memories and "sound bites" they would soon experience.

2. *Ongoing narration:* In a show structured like a revue, as, for instance, The Open Book's verse anthology, *Poetry in Motion,* each new section is introduced by the performers. Eye contact with the audience is frequent and ongoing. Never resort to the tedious convention of assigning a narrator to read the stage directions. Good playwrighting, combined with a scene synopsis in the printed program, should be sufficient to set each scene for the audience. To my mind, any script that requires an omnipresent scene-setting narrator is a poor candidate for readers theatre staging. A better reason for employing a narrator or narrators between scenes is to reestablish the cast's presentational relationship with the audience.

3. *Asides to the audience:* Ongoing eye contact occurs in anthology shows, where the performers basically appear as themselves, but even when "fourth wall" playscripts are mounted readers theatre–style, asides to the audience are permissible and often effective. Any universalized sentiment is fair game. For example, soon after Mason Miller enters in Robert Hawkins's play, **The End of a Line,** he says, "Whew! It's so humid! It gets hot in New York, but . . . wow! Not like this. Now I know what they're talking about when they talk about an Alabama summer!" In The Open Book's production, the latter sentence was delivered to the audience, to foreshorten the aesthetic distance between them and Mason.

Textual Analysis
What is the writer trying to say? How does each scene, each motivational unit, each sentence, each word contribute to the

author's overall intent? Thorough textual analysis, a hallmark of readers theatre, is essential before the artists can begin to decide how to present the work. In addition to the usual interpretive work practiced by professional actors and directors, additional systems and devices are employed in readers theatre.

1. *Actor's techniques:* The performer marks her or his script for rhythmic patterns and rate of delivery, dynamics and timbre, inflectional and tonal variety. In addition to— sometimes counter to—the author's punctuation, the actor "scores" the script for vocal variety, dramatic effect and narrative flow. Pause marks and various diacritical marks are available for these purposes.

A. *Pauses.* Stops and pauses, as signaled by periods, colons, semicolons and commas, are important breathing places for the reader, but an actor sometimes cannot effectively communicate complicated syntax to an audience without ignoring or modifying the author's original punctuation. Furthermore, some prose (e.g., by Samuel Beckett, Ray Bradbury, Charles Dickens, William Faulkner, Henry Fielding) is a challenge to any set of lungs to hold out till the next punctuated pause. A wise oral interpreter will mark such a script with commas, apostrophes or eighth-note-rest marks to indicate places where quick, non-interruptive breaths must be taken.

B. *Dynamics and force.* Gradations of volume and stress may be offset with sequential circled digits (①②③②) to designate a "ladder" that the voice must go up and/or down. Crescendos and diminuendos may be depicted as in music, with the letter "V" drawn elongated and sideways.

C. *Inflection* can be keyed with up- or down-aimed arrows (↗ ↘) drawn in the white space above the text. If a literary passage consists of an extensive list of clauses, arrows may be combined with sequential circled digits so a quick scan of the script will remind the reader of the demands on his voice during a difficult section of prose, so he or she will not start too high or low.

D. *Tonal links* are useful in passages of text that contain a long parenthetical clause. By marking the beginning and end of the clause either with up- or down-slanted arrows, the interpreter can pitch it differently than the surrounding matter. The change in vocal texture will enable the listener to follow the thought clearly.

E. *Vowel duration* is a choice that may be used to alter rhythm or to vary tonal color. A long vowel is displayed in the script with a horizontal line, or macron, above it; a short one by a bowl, or breve; an extremely abbreviated vowel by a single dot over it.

2. *Directorial techniques:* When a work of literature is being considered for readers theatre adaptation, a director should assess its potential for the creative use of various vocal effects.

A. *A cappella music.* Because several members of The Open Book are accomplished singers, unaccompanied music is featured in many of our shows, especially our adaptation of Daniel Pinkwater's popular children's book, *The Hoboken Chicken Emergency,* which, at the author's suggestion, was turned into a mixture of cantata and ballad opera.

B. *Choral speech.* Such pyrotechnic vocal effects as antiphonal speech, crossfading dynamics, contrapuntal or multi-rhythmic declamation and/or unison passages can create an oral interpretation experience tantamount to chamber music. But these techniques should be employed sparingly lest they swamp the work of literature (and the audience) in gratuitous virtuosity.

C. *Sound effects.* The frank theatricality of readers theatre allows the actors to produce a wide range of sound effects: animal sounds, bells, the sigh of the wind, thunder, etc. In addition to vocalizing, the performers also may drum

on stools or the backs of books, shuffle their feet, clap their
hands and so on.

Arranging the Stage Picture

Despite modifications worked by its essential simplicity and
presentationalism, staging readers theatre is basically the
same as traditional theatre. Scenery, costumes, sound and
lighting effects are generally minimalized, and scripts, stools
and music stands may or may not be in evidence, but the
philosophy governing set arrangement and patterns of blocking is identical.

Each literary work staged at The Open Book is evaluated
for its position along a stylistic axis that ranges from "strict
oral interpretation" to traditional theatricality.

Some fiction and most playscripts fall at the latter end of
the spectrum and are staged similarly to other minimalistic
theatrical events. But most poetry and "language-rich" prose
are at the "interp" end of the axis. Such compositions are
best staged and blocked with extreme economy to permit the
audience to invest maximum creative concentration on the
author's sonority and imagery.

In the purest incarnation of "oral interp," a single reader
stands in one spot facing the audience, sometimes behind a
lectern, more often full front, book in hand. At the start of the
program, the book is closed; its opening is like raising the act
curtain. The reader introduces the literature, drops her or his
gaze to the book, opens it, raises her or his eyes and estab-
lishes direct contact with the audience, then begins to
"read." (Quotation marks offset the word "read" because by
performance time, the text must be memorized. Some readers theatre producers entirely dispense with onstage scripts,
but at least one book is always carried at The Open Book as a
symbol of the work being shared. Our final curtain call is
always reserved for the script itself.)

When the solo reader wants to distinguish a variety of

characters for the audience, he does so by "focusing" each along different fixed sight lines. Thus a performer reading the trial scene from Jerome Lawrence and Robert E. Lee's drama, *Inherit the Wind*, might, perhaps, look straight at the audience when narrating, turn his eyes and head several degrees to the left as he speaks Drummond's dialogue, or several degrees to the right when he portrays Brady.

A modified version of this technique is employed when more than one interpretive reader appears onstage.

From Page to Stage: Selecting and Adapting Literature for Readers Theatre

In her prefatory notes, Dr. Judy E. Yordon discusses some of readers theatre's variations and permutations, including performance art, to which I would add improvisational theatre. Despite this trend, in the foreseeable future, the interpenetration of readers theatre methodology into traditional theatre production will probably continue to derive chiefly from literature of all styles and genres, including prose, poetry, drama and nonfiction.

Although there are many worthwhile published readers theatre scripts now available, the response to the first three Open Book-*Fireside Theatre* competitions suggests that many dramatists still do not understand what readers theatre is all about and, even if they do, their expertise does not necessarily extend to the adaptation of nondramatic compositions.

To explore this topic thoroughly would take an entire book. Those who wish to do so should try Judy Yordon's *Roles of Interpretation* and *Readers Theatre Handbook* by Leslie Irene Coger and Melvin R. White. Presuming that the reader's chief concern is theatrical adaptation, I have bypassed the preparation of texts for solo oral interpretation in favor of a practical introduction to the problems and methods of dramatizing literature for ensemble readers theatre, as I

have encountered them during the past twenty years of pro-
ducing/directing at The Open Book.

General Advice

The chief premise of readers theatre is that the artists wish to
share literature they admire with the audience. Thus, it is
axiomatic that any work adapted for the form should resonate
with the adapter, director and readers. The degree of adaptation required to turn a literary composition into an effective
readers theatre script is unique to each case. While one
should remain as true to the original work as possible, it must
be kept in mind that the dramatic experience is time-bound
in a way that private reading of the same material is not.
Generally, the audience only gets to hear the composition
once, and cannot flip back to study a difficult passage. The
adapter must evaluate each work's scope and performance
accessibility, and prepare the final script according to these
criteria.

Theatre, like politics, is also an "art of the possible." Without adequate funding or a sufficiently-trained ensemble, it
would be purposeless to adapt, say, *Paradise Lost*. But as-
suming that the chosen literature fits the budget and suits the
skills of the available talent pool, the adapter's interrelated
duties are 1) to assess and develop the work's presentational
aspects, and 2) to evaluate the work's emotive and intellectual content and employ those techniques best suited to illuminate the text's latent dramatic experiences. Because readers theatre is a minimalist form that depends for its success
on actively engaging the audience's imagination, the adapter
will strive to accomplish her or his tasks as economically as
the work permits.

Some readers theatre authorities insist on bare stage,
stools and scripts without any scenery, special lighting,
sound effects or costuming, but The Open Book's position is
that the form is not compromised by the selective employ-

ment of theatrical elements. Thus, we will use tables, chairs, benches, cots, perhaps a portrait or other wall hanging, once in a while a freestanding set piece, such as a huge cactus in a play set in a New Mexico desert. Regarding lights, our performing space has two main rheostats so that the room's white light can be graded in intensity, which enables us to suggest daylight, twilight and nighttime without resorting, however, to traditional theatre's gel-tinted battery of fresnels and lekos. Sound effects? When the work is sufficiently presentational to permit the cast to reproduce them vocally, we do so; in more traditional plays, we eliminate nonessential sound effects, but those deemed indispensable are reproduced "live" offstage or via tape recordings. (Our narrators *never* read a sound effect ["We hear the whistle of a distant train . . ."], unless the noise occurs with the speech. Merely describing a sound effect, as is often the practice in staged readings, not only does not stimulate audience imagination, but compromises the performance's artistic truth.) As for costuming, works set in an historical period are always selectively "dressed."

Adapting literature for readers theatre requires familiarity both with traditional dramaturgy and some special techniques. Each work presents two related challenges, cultivating its presentational opportunities and developing the experience embodied in the author's text. Since each literary style contains its own unique problems, we will consider each individually. But remember, techniques discussed in one section may be equally effective in another mode.

Adapting Dramatic Literature

Turning a playscript into a readers theatre experience can be the easiest kind of adaptation task. The work, after all, was written to be performed and its dialogue has already been assigned to specific actors. Yet despite these advantages, not all theatre scripts are likely fare for readers theatre adaptation. Large-scale dramatic works like Shakespeare's history plays, which rely on spectacle and scope to embroil their characters in battle and pageantry strike me as poor candidates. So are works that require functional scenery to achieve key dramatic moments, as, for instance, the literally spectacular moment in Jerome Lawrence and Robert E. Lee's *The Crocodile Smile* when a group of "extras" swiftly build a theatre on a hitherto bare stage. Such works only can be adapted by sacrificing essential elements.

1. *Cast requirements:* The cast list of most plays is allocated on a one-for-one basis, that is, the author expects each character to be played by a different actor. Still, in plays with large casts it is common practice to assign two or more minor roles to the same actor, and it is sometimes possible to multiple-cast larger parts. In *Hamlet,* for instance, it is logistically and stylistically suitable to cast the same actor as both Polonius and Osric.

Logistics and style are the criteria for testing the necessary cast size of any playscript, whether or not it is to be produced for readers theatre. The economy of today's theatre forces producers to select works that require fewer paid performers. But while multiple casting is an attractive answer (especially to the actors), it is not always the best solution. At The Open Book, every submitted script, whether it be drama, prose or poetry, is considered in terms of its "irreducible cast size." In other words, how many interpretive artists are necessary to perform the work without compromising its dramatic impact? It would be possible, say, to produce Robert Hawkins's **The End of a Line** as an unblocked oral interpretation with one actor playing both sisters, establishing them "in space" by standing in one place and delivering each sister's speeches along a fixed sight line. For that matter, employing this technique, it would be possible for a single reader to perform all three roles. Possible, but not advisable, since the interaction of three distinct characters is vital to the artistic success of this play.

The Open Book's recent presentation of Constance Alexander's **Kilroy Was Here,** included in this volume, provided us with a casting challenge since the submitted script was "unvoiced," that is, no individual speakers were designated for any of it. Even a casual reading, of course, reveals a succession of dramatic monologues, some clearly meant to be spoken by one actor, some by another. There are also passages that relate to a person or persons who never reappear, such as the serviceman who began and ended the war with a hangover. Then there are the radio commercials, the "Loose lips sink ships" slogan and other sound bites. We decided to adapt the script for a six-person ensemble. Each actor consistently represented one member of the script's focal family (Johnny, his parents, two sisters and Uncle Augie) and were assigned various unrelated characters and audio bites.

Once the adapter has determined the minimum number of artists the script requires, he or she should give thought to the "mix" of the cast. No matter what role each performer is assigned to play, remember that he or she appears as a formalized version of her- or himself sharing the literature with the audience. Because each performer's "personal proof"— that is, the positive impression they make *as people* on the audience—is the producer's most important casting consideration, it follows that readers theatre is especially well suited to nontraditional or counter-casting. Provided there is a good stylistic reason for the choice, men can play women and vice versa, and racial barriers do not exist. Thus, in last season's production by The Open Book of Robert Hawkins's *Quiet! Three Ladies Laughing,* a mature black female appeared as the narrator, as Lou Berta, the family's maid, and also as Diedre, the little daughter of Ada Lou, a white woman. Late in the play, Diedre put her head in her Mama's lap—a dear, touching, wholly natural moment of theatre.

2. *Scenic and technical elements:* Decisions on how much or how little costuming, lighting, makeup, scenery and sound/special effects are needed should be put to the same test as cast size: what are the irreducible technical requirements? Readers theatre is an intimate art form, analogous to chamber music. The audience is expected to actively invest its creative imagination in the literature being interpreted, so, unlike traditional theatre, elaborate scenery and/or lighting may actually impede the success of the production.

To better understand this process, go to your local bookstore and purchase some of the classic radio dramas now available from several publishers. Turn off the lights and listen, perhaps, to the ultra-hardboiled eeriness of Carleton E. Morse's *I Love a Mystery.* Despite the sometimes improbable plots, the word pictures and judicious use of sound effects will build scenes in your mind more breathtaking than anything you've ever seen in the movies or on TV.

The Open Book's version of Constance Alexander's **Kilroy Was Here** employed six actors on stools with minimal blocking other than swiveling towards or away from the audience. Costumes were suggestive of the period, but not naturalistic; thus, Johnny did not change into a military uniform. On the other hand, last year's production of Jo Davidsmeyer's *Angel,* a portrait of the Ravensbruck concentration camp director Irma Grese, was fully dressed with British and German World War II military costumes. Blocking was elaborate with Irma's execution virtually choreographed.

In each of these instances, the same criterion held: how much or how little technical support enabled us to produce the script effectively without overstepping the parameters of readers theatre.

Obviously, these parameters are subjective. The producer (adapter, director) must decide whether the script would be better served as a fully mounted theatrical production. But remember, in readers theatre simplicity of presentation is an aesthetic, not an economic consideration. *Mise en scène* is never as important as the power of language.

3. *Presentational opportunities:* Plays with built-in presentational devices such as asides and soliloquies, narration and other varieties of audience interaction are likely candidates for readers theatre. Some of these techniques are commonly associated with Shakespeare, Molière and other "high-style" playwrights, yet one may also find imaginative presentational moments in works by contemporary playwrights as diverse as Samuel Beckett, Arthur Miller, Michel deGhelderode, Harold Pinter, Neil Simon, Tom Stoppard, Thornton Wilder and many others.

If a playscript meets other performance criteria, a "fourth wall" play still can be adapted for readers theatre, though its presentational aspects are likely to be minimal. For example, in Robert Hawkins's **The End of a Line,** its three characters meet and interact in a small home in Birmingham, Alabama. Their story is "discovered" by the audience as it peeps over that familiar invisible "fourth wall." At first glance, this script appears to present no presentational opportunities. However, when The Open Book staged it in New York, two presentational touches were added.

A. At the beginning, the lights discovered Nora knitting, while off to a side, on a stool, sat the actor assigned to play Mason Miller. He served as a master of ceremonies, announcing the title and author, then leading the audience into the world of the play by saying, "It's a hot day in Birmingham, Alabama. We are in the modest living room of a home shared by two sisters. Nora, the younger of the two, attempts to keep busy by working on her knitting, but she seems nervous. So is her sister Margaret, who comes into the room and starts straightening up, in preparation for a visitor." As he named Margaret, the actor playing her appeared and the play got under way as Mason swiveled upstage on his stool— a typical readers theatre exit.

B. At certain points in the script, the actors spoke directly to the audience. At one point, Margaret said, "Down here, Mr. Miller, we try not to air our dirty linen in public." With a distinctly unfriendly glance at one presumably liberal "Yankee" audience member, she spoke the next line admonishingly: "There are some things that should be kept . . . private." A line of dialogue that reveals or expresses a character's opinion, or voices a "universalized" dictum is generally effective when delivered presentationally, as, for example, Smirnov and Madame Popova, in Chekhov's *The Boor,* who may respectively rail to audience members of the opposite sex on the evils of Woman and Man.

Adapting Prose: General Advice

All prose is potentially adaptable. Short stories, novellas and portions of novels can become one-act plays or may be arranged as an anthology of related or contrasting material. Novellas and novels can be dramatically adapted to fill one or more full evenings. Essays, journalism, biography, etc., may be apt raw material for a dramatic monologue or ensemble anthology.

Despite this stated potential, some prose works are challenging to adapt because of excessive length, syntactical complexity, dense imagery, emphasis on internal monologue to the exclusion of character interaction, or any number of other factors. Still, successful scripts have been fashioned from such unwieldy material as John Dos Passos's *U. S. A.* and James Joyce's *Ulysses,* so anything is possible. But remember, whereas dramatic literature and poetry often can be adapted word for word, prose usually has to be streamlined. The adapter must decide when to remain faithful to the original text and when to simplify and/or condense. The adapter must consider a work's timing, both overall length (playing time) and the proportion of individual sections and must decide, on a case by case and word by word basis, whether

the author's syntax and diction need to be simplified in defer-
ence to audience comprehension.

Though one must be as faithful as possible to the original
text, one should never hesitate to tighten descriptive passages or inner monologue if their inclusion militates against
the performance's successful flow. (If the work is protected
by copyright, the adapter must not only obtain permission to
perform it, but will also probably have to secure the author's
permission before changing the work.)

Adapting Prose: Fiction

When preparing fiction for readers theatre adaptation, I
study the author's narrative style in order to assess the work's
inherent dramatic possibilities.

1. What is the story's viewpoint? A tale told in the first
person is easy to dramatize since it is being shared by a
character in the story with the reader (audience). A third-
person narrative presents a variety of choices and problems,
depending on whether the omniscient author stays "over the
shoulder" of a single character, or shifts from one to another,
and depending on how close he focuses on actions and
thoughts.

2. How much of the narrative is told through summary and
description? Such passages set mood and help the audience
visualize the action. They may be allocated to a narrator or
narrators or may be treated as internal monologues delivered
by characters as asides.

However, the adapter should remember that summary is
an epic device calculated to bridge time and sum up necessary, yet essentially unremarkable events. Too much of it
flattens both immediacy and dramatic impact, and the same
may be said of descriptive passages, no matter how beauti-
fully expressed. Employ them sparingly.

3. How much is scenic depiction? Physical action, dialogue and inner monologue comprise the heart of good drama distilled from prose.

Dialogue, of course, can and should be spoken, though not necessarily as fully as in the original work. John Hersey's *The Child Buyer* has been turned into a script of average length, but the original novel, written as a sequence of congressional transcripts, would require several days to perform uncut.

Physical action may be described or performed, depending on its nature and the constraints of physics. A makeup designer might replicate the look of Ray Bradbury's "illustrated man," but the character's animated tattoos could not actually come to life onstage.

Direct inner monologue refers to literally rendered thought, often offset in italics, as, *Sure hope she doesn't know how much I hate her new hair-do!* It is easily employed as dialogue, as Eugene O'Neill proved repeatedly. Indirect internal monologue, on the other hand, is filtered through the author's interposing voice. ("Harry hoped his wife didn't realize how much he hated her new hair-do.") It could be relegated to a narrator, but the adapter may wish to transform indirect thought into the more immediate and dramatic direct mode.

This again raises the question of how much of the work's original text the adapter ought to preserve. While it is improper to veer too far from the author's intentions, the adapter must bear in mind that the audience does not have the reader's advantage of pausing to reread a passage. All theatrical performances are time-bound; there is a limit to the powers of assimilation and, for that matter, patience, of even the most sophisticated audience. Sometimes the only way to preserve the author's intention is to *judiciously* edit the original. For instance, attributions most always can and should be cut. Unless one needs to preserve the rhythm of a passage of prose-poetry, there is no need to tell the audience "he said" or "she said" if the words are emerging from the mouths of the actors (characters) themselves.

Prose fiction can be adapted for readers theatre in the conventional fashion of one actor per character, or a system of multiple casting may be devised. The adapter may wish to assign a narrator or narrators to the passages of summary and description.

A useful way to stage prose fiction is to employ the so-called *chamber theatre* technique, in which each performer is responsible for her or his character's dialogue, plus all description and inner monologue pertinent to that character. Here is an example from The Open Book's adaptation of Daniel Pinkwater's *Blue Moose:*

THE MOOSE: Do you mind if I come in and get warm? I'm just about frozen. (*To the audience*) The moose brushed past him and walked into the kitchen. His antlers almost touched the ceiling. The moose sat down on the floor—

MR. BRETON: —next to Mr. Breton's stove.

THE MOOSE: The moose didn't move. Wisps of steam began to rise from his blue fur. After a long time the moose sighed . . . (*loud sigh*)

MR. BRETON: He sounded like a foghorn. (*Addressing the moose*) Can I get you a cup of coffee? Or some clam chowder?

Adapting Prose: Nonfiction

Nonfiction once was dismissed as unadaptable, but it is unlikely that anyone still holds that opinion. Autobiography, biography, essay, reportage and even some kinds of didactic prose can and have been successfully adapted into entertaining and often surprisingly dramatic works. Successful examples include Samuel Gallu's breezy portrait of President Harry S. Truman, *Give 'em Hell, Harry;* Fredd Wayne's elegant one-man play, *Benjamin Franklin, Gentleman;* last year's *Fireside Theatre*/Open Book competition winner *Memorial,* in which Charles LaBorde dramatized oral and written recollections of Viet Nam War veterans, and this year's co-winner, **The Most Dangerous Woman,** an emotionally charged show fashioned from the life and speeches of the colorful labor union organizer, Mother Jones. Each of these achieve their effects largely through well-chosen language and imaginative presentational elements, the two key characteristics of readers theatre.

Even though these examples indicate that drama can be created from nonfiction, it is a category that poses a difficult problem for the adapter, since the literary goals of biographers, essayists and journalists are generally unrelated to those of the dramatist. To design a show from a nonfiction work, or a series of related works, one must study the material to determine its theatrical potential. If it is dramatically viable, it will fall into one of three modes.

1. A dramatic monologue can be shaped from diaries, speeches, newspaper articles, etc., as in **The Most Dangerous Woman,** a show so language-rich and naturally presentational as to blur or even eradicate the line between traditional drama and readers theatre.

2. A dramatized version of the material may be arranged by creating a setting/occasion and a set of characters conducive to airing the author's thoughts. For instance, in The Open Book's *Six Women in Search of Liberation,* speeches by Sojourner Truth, Susan B. Anthony and other women's liberation personalities were devised as a platform meeting with the audience treated as if they were all suffragettes. Connective passages linked the various historical speeches, including a "dramatized" portion of Susan B. Anthony's trial for

"illegal" voting, and the rally ended with the cast leading the audience in an authentic protest song of the period.

3. A combination of the monologue and dramatic methods may be devised. Many years ago, the operatic/Broadway tenor Robert Rounseville commissioned me to create a one-man show based on the life and writings of the great British philosopher-mathematician Bertrand Russell. Unfortunately, Robert only lived long enough to perform a portion of the script at Deerfield Academy and Western Washington State University. After his unexpected demise, the Russell estate permitted me to revise *Bertrand Russell's Guided Tour of Intellectual Rubbish* as an ensemble piece for The Open Book.

Its succession of scenes on a variety of topics such as Education, Marriage and Morals, Religion and Science utilized various readers theatre techniques to bring this body of hard-to-dramatize material to life.

An ensemble of three men and three women was employed, five of whom remained behind the proscenium frame while the actor who portrayed Russell spoke to the audience from the auditorium floor, sometimes from behind a lectern, other times seated on the edge of the apron. Such presentational moments included monologues about Russell's childhood and advice on growing old, as well as a telephone conversation with a reporter, in which Russell gave his impressions of various famous statesmen and artists he met during his lifetime.

Sometimes the ensemble appeared with Russell, as in the Education sequence at the beginning of Act II. During the intermission, a blackboard was brought onto the auditorium floor. Russell began the proceedings in cap and gown and "chalktalked" to the audience. Then the ensemble took their places onstage as a classroom of students with whom Russell interacted, professor to pupils. In other sequences, the ensemble worked by itself, as in a poetic passage about comets, when they entered in choir robes and spoke in unison and antiphonally. In another place, the performers donned white lab jackets and fiddled with test tubes and beakers of liquid while they aired Russell's opinions about science. After a few moments, one of them poured the mixture they were concocting into several martini glasses. They all took a glass, sat down and continued the scientific discussion over cocktails.

Adapting Poetry

Poetry is perhaps the most challenging medium to adapt, but it can also be the most rewarding. Its heightened language, emotive imagery and metrical variety offer rich opportunities for dramatic, often pyrotechnical theatre.

Pure poetry is the topic of this discussion, not verse drama or poetic prose. Verse adaptation techniques can, of course, be applied to dramatic poetry and poetic prose, and vice versa. Still, one tends to adapt verse drama by playwrights like Dryden, Eliot, Marlowe, Rostand, Shakespeare, and so on, essentially the same way as one prepares any dramatic composition for readers theatre.

Similarly, the considerations and techniques that apply to prose fiction are valid for the poetic prose one encounters in authors like Conrad Aiken, Samuel Beckett, Ray Bradbury, William Faulkner or Thomas Wolfe. Thus, when Open Book charter member Parke Godwin prepared for our ensemble an authorized adaptation of a portion of Edna Ferber's novel, *Show Boat,* he arranged it for six voices in a format virtually indistinguishable from such narrative poetry as, say, Robert Frost's "The Death of the Hired Man," a work frequently adapted for readers theatre since so much of it is direct dialogue.

An adapter preparing prose or narrative poetry must not interfere with the work's rhythm, structure or imagery. One cannot trim lines from a sonnet, since it must be fourteen lines in length. Attributions, often cut from adapted prose fiction, may be necessary to preserve tone or meter, as in this passage from **Kilroy Was Here,** as adapted for The Open Book:

FIRST WOMAN: I counted stars on the way to school every
   day.
   Blue stars. One, two, three. I thought they were beautiful.

SECOND WOMAN (*Mother*): We had one in our window for
   Johnny.

FIRST WOMAN: One day I saw the Lawson's down the street
   got a gold one. I ran home and told my mom
   I wanted a gold one, too. She slapped me.

SECOND WOMAN (*Mother*): And then she cried.

FIRST WOMAN: Grandma told me later
   you had to earn a gold star.

THIRD WOMAN (*Grandma*): A blue star means a soldier's
   far away from home. A gold star means he's gone to
   heaven.
   A blue star's better,

FIRST WOMAN: she said.

"Voicing" Poetry for Readers Theatre

Whether the adapter is preparing prose or poetry, the first task is to decide on the size and variety of ensemble neces- sary to do the work justice. The adapter must analyze the poem's viewpoint. Is it wholly expressed in the omniscient third person (the author's voice) or is some of it spoken (overheard) by named, or implied characters? The viewpoint should suggest the number and type of readers needed.

1. *Cast size:* Much of **Kilroy Was Here** consists of speeches by "real" people, though not all are given names: a mother and father, their son Johnny and their two daughters, one of whom is the work's principal narrator, Uncle Augie and Grandma, but there are also other characters: the pinsetters at the bowling alley, the serviceman with a hangover, the boy who delivers the telegram. There are indirectly described people, such as the stateside college professors. There are also radio announcers and anonymous voices for sound bites like "Loose lips sink ships." The sonority and flow of **Kilroy** suggested that Father, Johnny and Uncle Augie had to be three distinct voices. As for the women, there are a few speeches by Grandma, but she is not an ever-present personality like Mother and was ultimately assigned to the actor playing the younger sister, who thus played the oldest and youngest family members. Each subsection of the script was reviewed to see if an ensemble of three men and three women could cover the six main characters, the extras and the sound bites without confusing overlapping of identities.

2. *Pitch and timbre:* Nowadays, choice of cast is a directorial concern, or in the case of much professional theatre, a matter of selection by committee with playwright, producer, director and other artists often involved. Historically, playwrights from Sophocles, Shakespeare, Molière and W. S. Gilbert tailored their work to the skills (and presumably the limitations) of an ongoing ensemble.

The readers theatre adapter does well to follow the latter approach, voicing scripts for the best available members of the talent pool. As in all theatre, one shapes each role to the respective emotive skills of each artist, but the preparation of an effective readers theatre script also lays special stress on the cast's vocal characteristics. What is the ensemble's collective tonal range? What is each actor's pitch, timbre and tessitura? Will their voices blend well in concerted passages? Proper voicing of poetry adapted for readers theatre requires the ear of a trained musician.

The cast of **Kilroy Was Here** was preselected for vocal pitch, timbre and range. The deepest voice was Father's; Johnny and Uncle Augie were higher, while the women, highest to lowest, were the youngest daughter, Mother and the narrator, who was "scored" at the middle of the ensemble's register. Their varying timbres might be described as flute (youngest daughter), oboe (Mother), cello (the narrator), violin (Johnny), tenor sax (Augie) and organ (Father).

In an anthology script of poetry, pitch and timbre may enable an adapter to evaluate which passages should be solos, which duets and which are best for three or more voices. (Other factors may affect this decision: the work's diction, syntax, rhythm, sonority, imagery, etc.)

Ultimately, the adapter must develop her or his taste and learn to trust it. Sometimes the best adapting choice will be obvious; sometimes it will be necessary to experiment and revise; sometimes a passage may work well several ways.

For instance, this sonnet from The Open Book's anthology script, *Poetry in Motion*, is effective as a solo piece, but "works" better as a duet for "cello" and "English horn," that is, a man and woman with similarly pitched voices, but differing in timbre.

MAN: I searched the beach to seek a perfect shell,
But only found those chips and bits that fell
Where hungry seagulls hurled them high to land
At morning tide upon the salt-smacked sand.
My mind that perfect shell could clearly see—
In vain, my eyes did seek its symmetry.

So, since I cannot bring that gift to you,
I hope this crafted shell of words might do.

WOMAN: Like shells, our souls at birth are whole and free,
But all too soon are stolen from the sea,
And though the heart a noble start has planned,
Too often it lies broken on the sand.

BOTH: Then let us lie, who love each other well,
And say we see in each a perfect shell.

The tone of another sonnet from the same script is neither
lyrical nor romantic, but whimsically didactical. The orches-
tration used in the former poem was deemed inappropriate;
it was "scored," instead, for a high, fluty woman's voice (FIRST
WOMAN); a deeper contralto (SECOND WOMAN) and a man's
voice, which, though lower in pitch than the two women, was
still lightly textured. This voicing was intended to point up
the work's wry pedantry. As you read it, imagine the tonal
contrasts.

FIRST WOMAN: Good poetry requires a sense of form.

MAN: Pure sound and sense alone won't make less worse
A banal batch of limply-metered verse,

SECOND WOMAN: Or rhyming, wretched doggerel transform.

MAN: Now if to Petrarch's rules you would conform,

FIRST WOMAN: A sonnet must not be too long or terse.
It must consist of fourteen lines; what's worse,
Each line must fit a rhyme scheme uniform:

SECOND WOMAN: Your first and fourth and fifth and eighth must
match,

MAN: Your last six lines contain three separate rhymes,

FIRST WOMAN: Your sixth and seventh echo two and three.

MAN: Now there's a special beat your craft must catch,

FIRST WOMAN: And you must do it fourteen different times:

ALL: daDEE, daDEE, daDEE, daDEE, daDEE.

Special Vocal Effects
There are many vocal effects possible when arranging a work
for readers theatre. Some have already been alluded to; others appear below. But let the user beware. In one of his Nero
Wolfe mysteries, Rex Stout observed that a man who writes
books is beset with innumerable temptations, and the same
may be said of readers theatre adapters when they employ
"special effects." Like a rich dessert or fine brandy, the techniques can be delicious, intoxicating or cloying. All are capable of producing moments of pure theatrical magic; all of
them, if abused, can also be pretentious.

Antiphony is the opposition of blocks or bodies of sound to
produce dramatic and tonal contrasts and harmonies. In the
manner of a *concerto grosso,* in which smaller and larger
bodies of musicians alternate playing a single composition,
the adapter achieves dramatic variety by assigning sections
of text to different numbers of performers: solo, duos, trios,
quartets, etc. One may also divide a larger ensemble into two
or more sections that sometimes speak in unison and sometimes in smaller groups, as in the choral sequences of the
Greek dramas, which are often antiphonal.

The passage below by Charles Lamb from The Open Book
script, *Poetry in Motion,* is antiphonal. It was performed by
five readers, two of them men, three of them women. Note
the alternation of solo passages and *tutti* as well as the voic-

ing contrast of three speakers, each of whom had differing vocal qualities. The first was a woman with a fluty voice, the fourth and fifth were men, a "cello" and "oboe," respectively.

FIRST READER: I have had playmates. I have had companions
    In my days of childhood, in my joyful school days.
    All, all are gone . . .

ALL: The old familiar faces.

FIFTH READER: I had a friend, a kinder friend had no man.
    Like an ingrate,
    I left my friend abruptly. Left him to think on—

ALL: The old familiar faces.

FOURTH READER: I loved a love once, fairest among women.
    Closed
    Are her doors to me. I must not see her. All, all are
    gone—

ALL: The old familiar faces.

As adapted by The Open Book, the coda of the Kelvinator ad in **Kilroy Was Here** explored the dynamic and tonal contrast of three female and three male voices by working them antiphonally.

WOMEN: For we believe all of us owe
    to those who have fought and worked to preserve it,

ALL: a strong, vital and growing America—

WOMEN: Where every man,

MEN: Every woman,

ALL: will have the opportunity
to make their dreams
come true.

Augmentation is a way of building volume or dramatic
force by adding voices to a passage that might otherwise be
spoken by a single reader. Here is an example from The
Open Book's two-man, three-woman version of Vachel Lindsay's poem, "The Santa Fe Trail":

FIRST MAN: Cars from

SECOND MAN: Chicago, Hannibal, Cairo.

FIRST MAN: Cars from

SECOND MAN & FIRST WOMAN: Alton, Oswego, Toledo.

FIRST MAN: Cars from

SECOND MAN, FIRST & SECOND WOMEN: Buffalo, Kokomo, Del-
phi.

FIRST MAN: Cars from

SECOND MAN, ALL THREE WOMEN: Lodi, Carmi, Loami.

"Bowing" indicates tonal flow. The adapter points up
places in the text where he feels there should be an inflectional or tonal pause, or ongoing flow without pause. Both
instances were used for tonal contrast in Francis Bourdillon's
poem, "Light," a sequence from *Poetry in Motion* arranged
for five readers. The soloists are both female; the first is a
"flute," the second an "English horn." Antiphony is also employed here, but "bowing" instructions occur in the third
lines of each stanza; the first tells the ensemble they should

xlvi   FROM PAGE TO STAGE

pause briefly between "light" and "of." The second indicates the line should flow without interruption. (The ensemble also applied contrasting tonal colors to these lines. The word "light" was spoken brightly, while the second verse line was afforded a "warmer" sound.)

ALL: The Night has a thousand eyes,

FIRST READER: And the Day but one;

ALL: Yet the light—of the bright world dies
   With the dying sun.

The mind has a thousand eyes,

SECOND READER: And the heart but one;

ALL: Yet the light
                of a whole life dies
   When love is done.

Five voices differentiating these lines in this fashion helped illuminate the poem's emotional burden.

Broken syntax refers to the distribution of individual sentences or stanzas between two or more readers. Every adapted work is divided into a variety of sentences assigned to the actors for whom each is most appropriate. "Broken syntax" takes the process one step further by dividing individual sentences into components to be distributed to a number of voices. By providing tonal contrast, this technique rests the audience's collective ear and helps them follow complicated thoughts by breaking text into pieces that can be tonally highlighted.

Commas and other punctuation stops provide logical spots to subdivide a text, as in this portion of the "meatless sausage patty" recipe from **Kilroy Was Here,** arranged for three women by The Open Book:

SECOND WOMAN: Mix the oats,

FIRST WOMAN: salt,

THIRD WOMAN: sage,

SECOND WOMAN: and eggs;

THIRD WOMAN: Form into four flat patties.

If a sentence is unusually long, or if the adapter sees a reason to modulate its tone, its syntax may be broken at places other than those stops provided by the author. A simple example of this appears above in the section on *Augmentation.*

When one chooses this option, it is important for the cast to function as a single organism. To guarantee even flow, in rehearsal I tell the cast they must be one actor with many heads. Each "head" must breathe with and subvocally speak every word in unison with each actual speaker, only "turning up the volume" when it is her or his time to talk. In **Kilroy Was Here**'s Kelvinator ad, broken syntax was employed for comic effect by splitting the text between two men. The main body of the ad was delivered in fulsome bass tones; the product name was spoken by a smiling second reader brightly and brassily:

FIRST MAN: The heart of your postwar kitchen
   will be

SECOND MAN: Kelvinator

FIRST MAN: electrical appliances.
   The new

SECOND MAN: Kelvinator

FIRST MAN: refrigerator.
   The new

SECOND MAN: Kelvinator

FIRST MAN: electric range.
   The new

SECOND MAN: Kelvinator

FIRST MAN: electric water heater.
   This is no dream.

Counterpoint is a musical device for combining two or more melodies into an harmonious whole. In readers theatre, one may split parts of a work into two or more sections to be read simultaneously by as many readers as necessary. This section of Vachel Lindsay's "The Santa Fe Trail" was arranged for two men and three women:

FIRST WOMAN: Listen to the quack-horn, ripping, racking (*Keep repeating*)

SECOND WOMAN: Listen to the crack-horn, slack and clacking (*Keep repeating*)

FIRST MAN: Way down the road, croaking like a toad—

SECOND MAN: Here comes the snarl-horn, brawl-horn, rude-horn (*Keep repeating*)

THIRD WOMAN: Followed by the prude-horn, oo-OO-oo horn
(*Keep repeating*)

FIRST MAN: Some of them from Kansas, some of them from Kansas.

(*First Woman stops*)

SECOND MAN: Here comes the hod-horn, plod-horn, sod-horn.

THIRD WOMAN: Never more to roam-horn, very-far-from-home horn.

FIRST MAN: Some of them from Kansas, some of them from Kansas,

SECOND MAN (*singing softly*): Far away the Rachel-Jane

FIRST MAN & THIRD WOMAN (*singing softly*): Not defeated by the horns
(*Second Woman stops*)
Sings amid a hedge of thorns . . .

Note how the sounds build until four separate lines run simultaneously and note the places where each one stops. In this passage, the first man never participates in the counterpoint, but balances the four readers antiphonally.

It should be remembered that in this and all of the examples in this chapter, the script was arranged for a vocally-balanced ensemble so that the director could make use of an effective vocal range and a palette of tonal colors.

Diminution, the opposite of augmentation, refers to the subtraction of voices from concerted passages to decrease volume and/or dramatic force. In this excerpt from *Poetry in Motion* derived from Swinburne's "The Garden of Proserpine," diminution points up the poem's bleakness. The ensemble consisted of one man and two women.

ALL THREE: From too much love of living,
   From hope and fear set free
   We thank with brief thanksgiving
   Whatever (*Second Woman turns upstage*)

MAN & FIRST WOMAN: gods may be
   That no life lives forever;
   That dead men rise up never;
   That even the weariest (*First Woman turns upstage*)

MAN: river
   Winds somewhere safe to sea. (*He turns upstage*)

In this passage, note how diminution is combined with *broken syntax* to achieve the effect of the voices "bleeding" into silence. Remember that turning upstage is generally tantamount to exiting.

Echoic effects are those in which words or parts of sentences are repeated like echoes. This device in the "loose lips" section of **Kilroy Was Here,** as adapted by The Open Book, was intended to suggest how rumors "get around."

MAN (*whispering throughout sequence*): Loose

WOMAN (*whispering throughout sequence*): Loose

MAN: Loose

WOMAN: Loose lips

MAN: lips

WOMAN: lips

MAN: lips sink

WOMAN: sink

MAN: sink

WOMAN: sink ships

MAN: ships

WOMAN: ships

MAN: ships

Layering is a variety of counterpoint that sets dynamic levels and/or disparate rhythms against one another, often balancing them in intensity, sometimes crossfading them. It is a demanding technique that requires considerable rehearsal to master. Several devices occur in the following example, an *a cappella* musical portion of *Poetry in Motion*. A solo voice begins, then four voices are layered one upon the other, after which three voices sing together while the fourth continues to sing contrapuntally. Next, all five sing together and, lastly, the first voice reappears antiphonally and in diminution.

FIRST MAN (*baritone*): These are the cries of London-town:
　Some go up-street and some go down . . .

FIRST WOMAN (*lyric soprano*): Oysters, fresh oysters, fresh
　Wellfleet oysters.
　Periwinkles, periwinkles, mussels, cockles, sprats.
　(*Keeps singing these lines softly*)

SECOND WOMAN (*contralto*): Buns, buns, hot cross buns.
　If you have no daughters, give them to your sons.
　(*Keeps singing these two lines softly*)

THIRD WOMAN (*dramatic soprano*): Who'll buy my roses?
 Who'll buy my posies?
 Who'll buy my lilies, ladies fair?
 (*Keeps singing these two lines softly*)

SECOND MAN (*tenor*): Will you buy any tape or lace for your
 cape,
 My dainty duck, my dear-a?
 Any silk, any thread, any toys for your head,
 Of the newest and finest wear-a?

SECOND MAN, FIRST & SECOND WOMAN: Will you buy any tape
 or lace for your cape,
 My dainty duck, my dear-a?
 Any silk, any thread, any toys for your head,
 Of the newest and finest wear-a?

ALL FIVE: Come to the peddler! Money's a meddler!
 Money, money, money, money, money's a meddler
 That must mix in all men's ware-a!

FIRST MAN: These are the cries of London-town . . .

Onomatopoeia refers to the correspondence of certain words to natural sounds with which they are associated, such as that breakfast trio, "snap, crackle and pop." An example of engineered onomatopoeia occurs in an already-quoted passage from Vachel Lindsay's "The Santa Fe Trail." The readers are meant to imitate the sounds suggested by the italicized words. (Though "prude" is not onomatopoeic, its vowel contains the same prissy quality as the ensuing "oo-OO-oo," and was played accordingly. Similarly, the assonance of the next-to-last line suggests heaviness. The vowels in the final line are not onomatopoeic, but were stressed to conform to the rest of the sequence.)

> Listen to the *quack*-horn, ripping, racking . . .
> Listen to the *crack*-horn, slack and clack-
> ing . . .
> Here comes the *snarl*-horn, brawl-horn, rude-
> horn . . .
> Followed by the *prude*-horn, oo-OO-oo
> horn . . .
> Here comes the *hod*-horn, *plod*-horn, *sod*-
> horn . . .
> Never more to *roam*-horn, very-far-from-*home*
> horn.

Note that in the first and second lines, other words—ripping, racking, clacking—are also onomatopoeic. They were not stressed because it was felt that more than one such sound per line would provide too much counterpoint and drown out the solo reader. Also notice the accenting of more than one word in the last two lines. By this time, other voices had dropped out, so there was no problem of balance. The accented vowels in these two lines helped slow the tempo.

Slowing the tempo is another possible special effect, as is acceleration of delivery. One might also indicate changes in dynamics or rhythm. The special vocal effects possible in readers theatre are probably only limited by the imagination of the adapter.

KILROY WAS HERE

A Spoken Opera

by Constance Alexander

Tied for first place in The Open Book/*Fireside Theatre*'s second readers theatre competition is **Kilroy Was Here**, "a spoken opera" in one act by Constance Alexander. An excellent example of a free verse readers theatre script, it neither specifies the size nor gender of the cast, and even leaves assignment of individual speeches entirely up to the performing artists.

A former resident of Metuchen, New Jersey, Constance Alexander moved in 1988 to Murray, Kentucky where she lives with her husband.

The Open Book production of **Kilroy Was Here** opened October 12, 1995, as part of "American Time Capsules," a show that also featured another of Ms. Alexander's scripts, *'64 Blue Letters*, and a readers theatre arrangement of Conrad Aiken's poem, "Mayflower." The New York cast of **Kilroy Was Here** included:

FIRST MAN	Toby Sanders
FIRST WOMAN	Emily Blake
SECOND MAN	Wayne Markover
SECOND WOMAN	Karen Cressman
THIRD MAN	R. Mack Miller
THIRD WOMAN	Jennifer Daniels

The stage is dark. The only sound is 1940's hit parade music that fades to sounds of a crowd as the lights come up.

This is before the war.
A picture of me on Memorial Day, 1941.
Holding an American flag.
One of those little flags that's just
the right size for a two-year-old.
I am dressed like a rosebud,
wrapped in pink crepe paper
so I can be a flower at the grave
of the Unknown Soldier.
My brother is holding a wooden rifle,
and my mother is squinting into the sun,
her mouth open, her hand shading her eyes,
nearly a salute. Seven months later
there will be war and another baby,
and my father will sign up,
but today there's a picnic to be had,
and speeches in the park. Everyone will wave
those little flags that are made in Japan
and there will be pictures, pictures and more pictures.
My father takes the same shot two or three times,
warning us not to move. Insurance, he calls it,
in case someone's eyes are closed.

*   *   *   *   *   *

December 7, 1941. We were at a hockey game at
Madison Square Garden and this voice
came over the loudspeaker:

A naval engagement is in progress off the coast of Hawaii.
At least one enemy aircraft carrier has been sighted in
    action
against the Pearl Harbor defenses.

Hawaii?

What Pearl Harbor defenses?

Where's Pearl Harbor?

A few minutes later another voice
comes over the P.A.

The Japanese have bombed the U.S. military base at Pearl
    Harbor,
Hawaii. All servicemen are to report to their military
    bases.
I repeat. All servicemen are ordered to report to their
    bases
immediately.

For a second everything is still.
Silent.

And then the boys in uniform begin to file out. They look
    so
young.

One person starts to clap.

And then another.

And another.

The way the stars come out.

One here.

One there.

All of a sudden
hundreds. Thousands.

They got a standing ovation.

I've never seen anything like it.
Before or since.

            *   *   *   *   *   *

Don't know who had the camera,
or why—of all things—we were
having our picture taken.
It could've been a shot
of the Eastside Kids.

We made rude faces at the camera,
sneering like Humphrey Bogart or
John Garfield in a gangster film.

"Tough guys" we call ourselves,
wearing our hats backwards
and slouching in that way that drives
teachers wild.

We are pinsetters in a bowling alley.
1941. Picking up spare change and praying
that one of them Betty Grable blondes
will pick us up. This is December 7,
right after word came.

If the recruiting office was opened,
we would've enlisted on the spot.
That's what we all kept saying anyhow.

We got copies of the picture made,
one for each of us. Eight of us that day.
Eight. Half as many four years later.

            *   *   *   *   *   *

We were sitting at the kitchen table.
My father was carving a chicken for Sunday dinner
and mother was making gravy.

Seems like she was always making gravy. With lumps.

Uncle Augie came barging through the front door
like Hitler was after him.
"They bombed us in Hawaii," he kept shouting.
"It's war!"

Dad turned on the radio right away.
My little sister, Sylvie, kept asking,

"When is 'The Shadow' on, Daddy?
I wanna hear Lamont Cranston."

My father shot her a look
stopped her dead in her tracks.

Mom didn't take off her apron
the rest of the day.
But we never did sit down
to a proper meal.

Johnny kept saying he wished he was 18
so he could join the Army and fight the Japs.
Making varsity basketball didn't seem so important
anymore, he said.

I feel like I grew up December 7, 1941.

It was the first time in my life
I saw my father break down and cry.

*   *   *   *   *   *

I don't want to hear another word about the Army,
young man. Not 'til you graduate high school.

You heard your mother. Not another word.

*   *   *   *   *   *

Me, I was trying to hitch a ride back to the base.

Me, I was trying to hitch a ride back to the base.
Wasn't nowhere near a radio, so what did I know?
I was out with my buddies the night before,
and all I could think about
was this godawful hangover.
Couldn't figure out why people
was treating me like I'm
something special.

Wasn't long after Pearl
I was on my way to the South Pacific myself.
For me, the war started
with the worst hangover
of my life. Come to think of it,
that's how it ended too.

*   *   *   *   *   *

At school the next day,
they let us listen
to President Roosevelt's speech.
It came at noon,
and you couldn't hear a sound in the lunchroom.

Except for Wally Horner taking a bite
out of a big, red Macintosh apple.

(*From Roosevelt's
declaration of war,
December 8, 1941.*)

"Yesterday, December 7, 1941—a date which will live in
    infamy—
the United States of America was suddenly and
    deliberately
attacked by naval and air forces of the empire of Japan."

He asked Congress to declare war.

All hell broke loose.

It lasted for five or six minutes.

And then the cry rose from the joint session.

Vote!

Let's vote.

We were at war.

Just like that.

* * * * * *

One day my brother and me were looking
for pine cones to decorate the house for Christmas.
The next day we were at war.

Had our first air raid drill
at the end of school that day.
The teachers told us
to practice running all the way home
in case of an enemy attack.

"Run like the wind, children."

I never was so scared in my life.
Next four years I worried
about not being home if the war came right
to our town. How would I find my mother
if I was at school?

What if Daddy is at work and can't get home
to help us?

* * * * * *

What if Johnny just decides to sign up
on his 18th birthday? They can't do anything.

Mama'll kill him.

* * * * * *

My dad is an Air Raid warden.
Has a special hat. And a big flashlight.

"Lights out! Lights out in there!
Don't you know there's a war on?"

* * * * * *

My sister and I will hide in Mama's closet
if we're invaded. Way in back.
Behind all the hat boxes.

Even Mama can't find anything in there,
so how can the Japs find us?

* * * * * *

She wouldn't even say goodbye to Johnny.
And he looked so handsome in his uniform.
Tall. Even taller with his cap on.
Those white teeth.
She wept in her bedroom
'til he was on his way out the door.

"Goodbye, Mom. I love you."

He called up the stairs to her.
Then he went up.
Tapped on the door. Lightly.
With one finger.

"It's something I gotta do, Mom.
I wouldn't've graduated anyway.
Not with my grades in English."

* * * * * *

The first time we got V-Mail,
she wouldn't open it.

It was black-bordered, grey.
Who could blame her?

Dear Folks, How is everything at home?
Fine, I hope. I am ok.

Johnny started every letter the same.

Dear Folks, How is everything at home?
Fine, I hope. I am ok.

Just like that.
Like he was working at a job
in a distant city. Pittsburgh, maybe.
Where he carried heavy boxes late at night,
and made friends with boys from Brooklyn
and Wyoming.

So long, Johnny,
he signed them.

In between "Dear Folks" and "So long,"
were remarks about the weather. The food.
How much he missed this or that
at home. The lumps in Mom's gravy.
Taking out the garbage.

He joked about the women
everywhere he went.

"He's going to get involved. I just know it."

Mother said this with raised eyebrows
and a sigh, resigned to a girl
who chewed gum and showed her underpants
when she danced the jitterbug at the USO.

These Texas women are really good looking,
and always wanting you to marry them.

That was at Camp Swift.

Then he went to Tennessee, Camp Forest.

It's way down in the mountains,
and these li'l ole mountain gals say,
'Whar ya'll goin'?'

Mother cringed at the thought
of a girl hillbilly. Us being
from the city and all.

"As long as she has all her own teeth
and can read, I guess a girl hillbilly'll
be all right."

Again the raised eyebrows. The sigh.

"He could've passed English,
if he'd've tried. I just know
he could."

                    *   *   *   *   *   *

The radio is an altar
in the center of the parlor.
Fine mahogany, curved corners,
gentle ridges you can stroke without risking
splinters. The wood is that fine.

                    *   *   *   *   *   *

Do you think Gabriel Heatter
is really God? I do.
He's everywhere,
and on our side too.
His golden voice.

On summer nights
you can hear him,
a low hum floating
from every house,
spreading the word,
and sweet faith
in the Allies.

                *   *   *   *   *   *

Whistle while you work.
Hitler is a jerk.
Mussolini pulled his weeny,
and now it doesn't work.

                *   *   *   *   *   *

I drew pictures of Hitler
and hung them on a tree.
And then I threw stones.
The bigger the better.
Every time I hit him,
another German soldier died.
Amen.

                *   *   *   *   *   *

Loose
lips
sink
ships.

                *   *   *   *   *   *

Dear Folks, How is everything at home?
Fine, I hope. I am ok. I am sorry
I didn't write sooner. I'm a rifle expert now.
Got a medal and two bucks for being
3rd highest in the company.

"You're much too tall to be a sharpshooter,
Johnny. Tell them you're too tall."

                *   *   *   *   *   *

Worst licking I ever got
was over grandma's favorite skillet.
The one grandpa always said
she hit him with to make that scar
on his forehead.

"Now how'm I gonna make an omelet for Johnny
when he comes home," she said, "without my favorite
frying pan?"

Her voice fluttered like the needle of a compass.
No use telling her I also gave
my favorite Popeye windup toy.
Enough scrap to get me into the movies free.
A Roy Rogers double feature
and newsreels of Africa,
where Rommel the Desert Rat
tracked down my Uncle Augie like a dog.

*   *   *   *   *   *

Some of us spent the war at the movies.
Sometimes there were children
in the newsreels.
That's where my nightmares
came from. Children stacked
like cords of wood. Rooms full
of empty shoes. And eyeglasses.

*   *   *   *   *   *

Call for Philip Morris!

No curative power is claimed
for Philip Morris . . . but
an ounce of prevention
is worth a pound of cure.
Philip Morris are scientifically far less
irritating to the nose and throat.

When smokers changed to Philip Morris,
substantially every case of irritation of the nose or throat—
due to smoking—either cleared up completely,
or definitely improved.

Findings reported in a leading medical journal.

Far finer pleasure plus
far more protection.

Call for Philip Morris.

*   *   *   *   *   *

Slap
the
Jap
with
iron
scrap.

Burma
Shave.

*   *   *   *   *   *

There were shortages of everything.
Sugar.
Shoes.
Meat.
Tires.
Coffee.
Fat.
Butter.
Cheese.
The button makes it yellow
if you squeeze.

Delrich E-Z Color Pak
ends mixing bowl mess!

No wonder homemakers are thrilled
with Delrich E-Z Color Pak Margerine.
No mixing bowl. No messy dishwashing.
Delrich quickly blends to a luscious
golden yellow right inside the sealed
plastic pack. Treat your family
to Delrich E-Z Color Pak Margerine
today!

* * * * * *

Dear Folks, How is everything at home?
I am fine and hope you are the same.
It's my last day in the old U. S. of A,
and what a place to spend it. New York City.
It's been just like a movie all day. Everything's
so American! Took a walk this morning and could hear
jazz on someone's radio. Rode a train and saw a tractor
that said, "Made in Toledo," on the side. A billboard said,
"Try Kalladowsky's Steak House," and even that sounded
*   American.*
It got foggy toward dusk. When we pulled out of New York
*   Harbor,*
you couldn't even see the Statue of Liberty. Some fellows
stood on the bridge singing, "Harbor Lights." I can tell you
I wasn't the only one with a lump in my throat. God keep
*   you 'til*
I come back. Love, Johnny.

* * * * * *

Twinkle, twinkle little star,
Took her riding in my car.
What we did I ain't admittin',
But what she's knittin'
Ain't for Britain!

* * * * * *

Men in suits, wearing fedoras,
one of them smoking a pipe,
and all of them on bikes.

They look proud of themselves,
these college professors.
Peddlars of wisdom.
Their bit for the war effort
to foresake automobiles.
"To conserve precious petroleum,"
one of them says in the interview.
He is the one with the pipe, the jaunty one
who will lose his only son
on the Burma Road.

* * * * * *

*Dear folks. I am fine and hope you are the same.
How is everything at home? All we ever talk about is food.
How when we get home we're gonna have our favorite meal
every night. You wouldn't believe the women—*

—In Ireland he said he was looking for an Irish Rose.

"A Catholic," Mother said. "I could live with a Catholic.
Aunt Mary married a Catholic."

She was already crossing herself and finding a place
in her heart for Purgatory.

We have three kinds of weather here, Johnny joked.

Now that he was getting used to writing letters,
he found the sense of humor that used to
get him detention at school.

*Three kinds of weather. It is about to rain, or it is raining,
or it has just stopped raining.
Ha ha ha.
So long, Johnny.*

* * * * * *

The heart of your postwar kitchen
will be Kelvinator electrical appliances.
The new Kelvinator refrigerator.
The new Kelvinator electric range.
The new Kelvinator electric water heater.
This is no dream.
We believe your hope for a new and finer home
can and will come true.

Here at Kelvinator, when Victory is won,
all the new strength, abilities and skills born of war,
will be turned to production for peace.

This will be our part in the building
of a greater, happier nation.
For we believe all of us owe
to those who have fought and worked to preserve it,
a strong, vital and growing America—
where every man,
every woman,
will have the opportunity
to make their dreams
come true.

                    *   *   *   *   *   *

Cake makeup.
Eyebrow pencil.
Straight. Make it straight.
Careful, careful.

I dream of having one pair of silk stockings.
Just one pair.

Silk stockings? Our
silk stockings are parachutes
in Africa.

Don't you know there's a war on?

* * * * * *

You're out of order,
Mrs. Hoarder.
Uncle Sam's
gonna be mad
at you.

* * * * * *

Buy Jeeps, buy Jeeps,
Send thousands of Jeeps o'er the sea, the sea.
Buy Jeeps, buy Jeeps,
And bring back my loved one to me.

* * * * * *

I counted stars on the way to school every day.
Blue stars. One, two, three. I thought they were beautiful.
We had one in our window for Johnny.
One day I saw the Lawsons' down the street
got a gold one. I ran home and told my mom
I wanted a gold one too. She slapped me.
And then she cried. Grandma told me later
you had to earn a gold star. A blue star means a soldier's
far away from home. A gold star means he's gone to
    heaven.
A blue star's better, she said.

* * * * * *

Dwarfed by plump lilacs
already tinged with bronze,
we stand by the railroad tracks
to wave the POWs on to Iowa,
which will remind some of them
of home.

They wave back,
seeming almost to beckon.
We make faces, risk the goose step,
shout "Heil Hitler" in that way

comedians have. Right arm a stiff hypotenuse,
left index finger the mustache
that tickles Eva Braun.
His mistress. Mistress.
A new word learned in war
but only whispered.
"Heil Hitler," once again,
this time spitting as we say,
"Achtung," the only other German word
we know. Our mother would have scolded us
for standing so close to the tracks.

"Don't you know the Beckley boy got killed that way?"

Reminding us of a next door neighbor
we never knew, a boy who died of a cause
more natural than war, though war was all we knew,
like Roosevelt and Churchill. But the train.
The train of POWs. We would have died
had it stopped in our little town
where strangers were invited to supper.

My sister and I play a German-soldier-comes-to-dinner
    game.
Sometimes he falls in love with me;
sometimes my sister.
He is blue and silver, with stars on his hat,
like a bottle of Evening in Paris perfume.
He speaks broken English,
teaches us the words for mashed potatoes
and corned beef hash. The other words he whispers.
After dinner we sit on the porch
and imagine life after the war.
Amber waves of grain. Weeping willows.
Lilacs swollen with spring rain.

*   *   *   *   *   *

Johnny looked sheepish in his wedding portrait.
"Look what I did," he seems to grin and shrug.
Shame and swagger all at once.

He is not sure what mother will say,
him marrying an Italian girl
with eyes dark as olives.
And breasts. Breasts.
They are beautiful, he thinks,
but he would never say this. Even to her.
She is Catholic, after all, and would have
to tell the priest. We are Methodist.

Right now he won't think of how
to tell mother about the Pope,
Extreme Unction, and his young wife's
splendid breasts.

*   *   *   *   *   *

Meatless Sausage Patties

1 cup rolled oats
½ teaspoon salt
½ teaspoon sage
2 eggs, beaten
2 tablespoons butter
1 beef bouillon cube

Mix the oats, salt, sage and eggs;
form into four flat patties.
Fry in the butter until browned
on both sides.
In a kettle
or saucepan,
boil 1 quart water
and add bouillon cube.
Pour mixture over patties.

Simmer, covered,
for thirty minutes.

Yield:
4 servings.
Delicious!

*   *   *   *   *   *

He stood up to answer the phone
in a foxhole and a sniper got him.
That's what his buddy told us. On the phone in a foxhole.
Our Johnny. Maybe someday this will raise a rueful smile.
How like Johnny, we might say.
He loved to talk on the phone.
One time Daddy got so mad he pulled it
out of the wall because it was suppertime,
and no decent people talked on the phone
when dinner was on the table.

There is no mistaking this for V-Mail,
though it is grey, mottled,
like the ceiling in a summer hotel.
It comes fifteen minutes after the phone call,
delivered in the Model T the telegraph office
reserves for these unhappy tasks.
The boy apologizes, for it is dinnertime,
and our father is stubbornly carving a chicken
with tears in his eyes and the radio turned loud.

Mother is making gravy in the kitchen.
They go to the door together.
Mother pushes her hair away from her forehead
and looks back to the stove, frowning,
as if worried the gravy will get lumps
while they stand there.
The boy shoves the telegram at them.
Somewhere outside there's a game going on.

Kids laughing. Shouting. A boy yells,
"Run, run for it, Davey."
                    *   *   *   *   *   *

He never saw a flamingo.
Or a shooting star.
Mother's shoulders squared
with the memory of lactation.
At the funeral it looked like this:
she put one arm around my father,
the other around us.
She never flinched at the 21-gun salute,
taps, the flag folded into a star and folded again.

She dreamed of him all the time.
I dreamed of Johnny last night,
she wrote to her sister.
He was at home. He had been cut in two just below the
      arms.
I picked him up and told him I would always love him
and was so glad he came home. Then I woke up and
      remembered.

Til the day she died there would be a
fragility to her, a measured calm.
Even cancer she took silently,
shaking her head slightly as if she knew
all along, or suspected, that something star-shaped
was going to kill her.
She never met Carmella. The war bride.
There wouldn't have been much to say
without Johnny, Carmella's English being
what it was. After a couple of years,
the letters stopped coming.

Mother's last wish was to go to Hawaii.
She wanted to see Pearl Harbor,

she said. Where it all began.
Not Europe with its forests, silent and green.
She wanted beaches. Sky. A place where you
could see the stars.

* * * * * *

Daddy brought me home
a teddy bear from the war.
Big, brown and fuzzy.
Bigger than I was.
I named it Kilroy.
After "Kilroy was here."

When he gave it to me I hugged it,
because I was afraid to hug him.
Didn't even know him.
Until he showed up with Kilroy,
he was just a picture on the mantel.
A man they said was my father.
A man who'd never held my hand
or tucked me in to sleep.
In the picture he has a smart aleck grin on his face.
A smirk. The kind of look that gets you in trouble
at school. His eyes are sliding off to the left,
like he's watching a pretty girl go by.

I kissed the picture every night
and it became him. The glass is smooth, cool.
The edges of the gilt frame are sharp if I'm
not careful. I want to touch his ear. His real ear.
To feel its ridges and whorls, the fleshy lobe.
The ear does not frighten me. It's the ear I see
when he comes through the door bearing Kilroy.
My mother has fallen to her knees. She is crying
and holding her hands free, her fingernail polish
still wet. He tries to sweep us both into his arms,
but Kilroy is there. He finally sits down on the floor

with us so Mother can weep on his shoulder.
I can see his ear perfectly. The one from the picture.
I want to put my ear up to his,
to hear the South Pacific.
I touch it gently. Like it is glass.
I count the buttons on his jacket.
Some of them are smooth,
and some have eagles you can trace
with your fingertips.
And those little stars.

*   *   *   *   *   *

This is us before the war.
Memorial Day, 1941.
See the little flag?
Made in Japan.
A year later—less than a year—
you'd've been a traitor
holding one of those things.
But today, that day, I am a rosebud.
Wrapped in pink crepe paper
so I can be a flower at the grave
of the Unknown Soldier.
My brother is holding a wooden rifle,
and my mother is squinting into the sun,
her mouth open, her hand shading her eyes,
nearly a salute. Seven months later
there will be a war and another baby,
and my father will sign up.

But today there's a picnic to be had,
and speeches in the park. There will be pictures,
pictures and more pictures. My father takes
the same shot two or three times,
warning us not to move. Insurance, he calls it,
in case someone's eyes are closed.

THE MOST DANGEROUS WOMAN

A One-woman Play
in Two Acts

by Ted Eiland

Tied for first place in The Open Book/*Fireside Theatre*'s second readers theatre competition is **The Most Dangerous Woman,** a two act play by Ted Eiland about Mary Harris Jones (1830–1930), a feisty folk hero best remembered as Mother Jones, America's preeminent labor agitator and union organizer for more than fifty years.

Ted Eiland describes himself as "a retired radio and television executive who took up a second career as a university lecturer, having taught in the theatre arts department of Western Carolina University in North Carolina, and then I retired from that to try my hand at writing." He is currently a resident of Cocoa Beach, Florida.

The Most Dangerous Woman premiered on November 6, 1992, at the Surfside Playhouse, Cocoa Beach, Florida, starring Barbara Walker as Mother Jones. A subsequent production also starring Barbara Walker ran for several days beginning January 29, 1993, at the Melbourne (Florida) Civic Theatre.

The Open Book's New York production opened March 7, 1996, and starred Beverly Fite.

The curtain is always open. The stage has four different playing areas.

Upstage center is a platform representing the various venues from which Mother Jones makes her speeches. It is on a slightly higher level than the two platforms on either side.

On the upstage left platform is a long wooden table of the type used as counsel tables in courtrooms and congressional hearings. A dark wooden arm chair is at the table, facing the audience. An American flag on a floor stand is to the rear and right of the table.

On the upstage right platform is a small, simple hotel room with minimal furnishings: a single-mattress bed, a plain dresser with mirror, a straight-back wooden chair placed at a small desk.

The downstage playing area is bare for the full width of the stage.

Backdrops for the three upstage playing areas can be draperies or something of a nature chosen by the director or set designer. Whatever is chosen should be non-invasive.

The three upstage playing areas should remain blacked out until Mother Jones enters one of them. At that juncture the particular area is lighted. When she leaves, the area is blacked out.

The downstage playing area is constantly lighted.

As the lights go up, the stage is empty. Now the lights go up in the upstage left hearing room-courtroom area. A man's voice is heard on the speaker system.

VOICE: The Commission now calls Mrs. Mary Harris Jones! (*Mother Jones enters from stage right. She is a small, elderly woman, but she holds herself erect as she walks across the stage. She carries a file folder. She is wearing a plain but well-tailored, ankle-length, black dress with a white dickey front and chin-high collar fringed with white lace. Her round black hat is small with a narrow black ribbon wrapped around it. It is set squarely on her head. She also wears wire-framed granny glasses with round lenses. Her hair is white. Her costume is representative of the late 1800s or early 1900s. She has an unsmiling but pleasant expression on her face, and looks like everyone's idea of a grandma. Her posture and her gait, however, make no concession to age. There is somehow an aura of no-nonsense feistiness about her. She walks firmly to the upstage left platform, steps up on it and sits in the chair behind the counsel table. She looks straight out into the audience with an expectant and alert expression*) For the record, will you please state your name.

MOTHER JONES (*her voice is strong and well-modulated*): My name is Mary Jones.

VOICE: You are the lady that is known across the country as Mother Jones, are you?

MOTHER JONES: I am.

VOICE: Where do you live?

MOTHER JONES: I live in the United States. I live wherever there is a fight going on against the robbers: the steel mills of Pennsylvania, the coal mines of West Virginia, the cotton mills of Alabama. I have no particular residence.

VOICE: No abiding place?

MOTHER JONES: No abiding place.

VOICE: You may make your statement, Mrs. Jones.

MOTHER JONES: Thank you, Congressman. (*She takes a sheet of paper from the file folder and places it on the table*) Earlier, you heard testimony by Douglas Baer, National Chairman of the Coal Mine Operators Association. He said, if you remember . . . (*she picks up the sheet of paper and reads from it*) "The rights and interests of the laboring man will be protected not by labor agitators such as Mother Jones, but by the *Christian* men and women to whom God, in His infinite wisdom, has given control of the property interests of this country." (*She puts down the sheet of paper*) I don't think I need comment on the utter stupidity of these words. I will only point out to this Commission that these *agents* of the *Almighty* have seen men killed daily in coal mines that defy all commonsense rules of safety; have seen men crippled, blinded and maimed and then turned out to almshouses and on the roadsides with no compensation; left to stand on street corners with tin cups, begging pennies for their women and children. (*She pauses*) God Almighty, gentlemen! Go down through the coal fields of this nation and see the damnable, infamous conditions that are there! I look with horror when I see these conditions! It is the brotherhood of labor that seeks to remedy these wrongs and to fight against the Douglas Baers of this world! They need your help!

VOICE: Mrs. Jones, why are we having one strike after another in our coal mines? Why can't these miners do what they're paid to do and not cause such a ruckus?

MOTHER JONES: Congressman, I know you're from Vermont and probably have never seen the insides of a coal mine, but let me tell you something. Until you've seen a coal mine, been inside one, seen how these men risk their lives every time they go down in the mines, crawling through spaces hardly big enough for a cat to squeeze through; put their lives on the line twelve hours a day, seven days a week in one of the most dangerous occupations that exists in the world, and then get paid not in cash but in company scrip not enough to keep *you* in cigars for a week! All this on top of poor housing, inadequate medical attention, brutal mine guards and high company-store prices—until you've seen all *that*, you've got no right to criticize anything that miners do to keep body and soul together!

VOICE: Madam, I remind you you're talking to a United States Congressman!

MOTHER JONES: Congressman, I don't talk to you any differently from the way I've talked to the President of the United States and several governors and the heads of some of the biggest corporations in this country. If you don't like to hear the truth, maybe you better try some other line of work! (*She stands, steps down from the platform and crosses to down center*) When I first got into the labor movement back in 1871, I had no idea of the number of bastards I'd run across like Douglas Baer. Now, before we go any further, you'd better understand something about me. I'm not one of your sweet-talking, hoity-toity "little old ladies." I swear a lot. I long ago quit praying and took up swearing. (*Short pause*) I get more action from swearing. I was a schoolteacher before I joined up with the union, and most of the men I dealt with knew it. So if I wanted to be accepted by them they had to be free to cuss when I was around. The first thing I did was to learn to cuss. (*Short pause*) Fluently. (*Short pause*) Something else

I learned was you got to talk a language people can understand. The public is the sleepiest damn bunch you ever
saw. You've got to wake 'em up! Now, in this connection, I
should point out when I talk about being in the labor
movement I'm talking about being a union organizer. And
I'm proud to say that I was the first woman union organizer in the United States, and remained the *only* one for
many years. And I was a damn good one.

Some of you might be thinking that being a union organizer is a peculiar line of work for a woman. Well, it was.
Especially back in those years. But, you see, I used to be
married to a union organizer. George Jones. Met him just
a little before I started teaching school in Memphis, Tennessee. (*She smiles fondly*) Fine man, George was. Fine
man. I met him at the boarding house where I stayed in
Memphis, and married him two months later. That was in
the summer of 1860 when I was thirty years old. A certifi-
able old maid by anybody's standards of that day—except
my own. George was an iron worker, one of the top men at
the foundry. And in his spare time he was secretly a union
organizer. Unfortunately, not a very successful one. In
those days the South was violently hostile toward unions,
even more so than today. And that included not just the
industrialists but the general public, as well. I didn't have
sense enough to realize that George was constantly in dan-
ger, because the very least that would have happened to
him if the company had found out that he was an organizer
would have been a beating. I mean a real beating. The
kind that some men never recover from. But George never
let it worry him. And nobody at the plant ever turned him
in, even though he had talked with practically every man
there, at one time or another, about joining the union.

Anyhow, I quit teaching and became a housewife. A year
later the Civil War broke out and George and I found

ourselves in an impossible situation. We both opposed
slavery, but with the war going on we didn't dare open our
mouths. Not in Memphis. For the four years of the war we
never allowed ourselves to get sucked into any kind of a
political discussion, especially about slavery. And for
someone with my big mouth, that wasn't easy.

George, meanwhile, worked like a mule, twelve-fourteen
hours a day, seven days a week, helping turn out guns and
other war material. It was a hectic time, but with it all we
started raising a family. Don't ask me how we squeezed it
in, but we did.

When the war ended in 1865, we had two beautiful little
girls. During the next two years two little boys came along.
It was a lovely family, and George and I couldn't have
been happier. (*She pauses, looks down for a moment, then
looks up*) In the summer of 1867, the weather turned almost unbearably hot, and Memphis was suddenly swept
by one of the most devastating yellow fever epidemics in
its history. People didn't just get sick. They died. By the
hundreds. It was like the city had been struck by one of
the plagues from the Middle Ages. The worst hit were the
poor neighborhoods where there were open sewers and
tainted water. But even the better neighborhoods suffered.
The difference was that the better-off people were able to
bury their dead in cemeteries, with some dignity. In the
run-down section of the city, where the poor lived, horse-
drawn wagons moved slowly down the streets while the
driver yelled, "Dead wagon! Dead wagon! Bring out your
dead!" From various houses along the street, doors would
open and surviving family members would struggle out to
the wagon carrying the dead body of a child or an adult.
Grief was everywhere as the bodies were placed in the
wagon to join God knows how many other victims, then

covered over with a heavy tarpaulin and taken away to be cremated.

George and I were terrified, not for ourselves but for the children. They were not allowed out of the house, even for an instant, poor things. July and August went by and we all stayed well. And we began to hope. (*Now a long pause as she stares over the heads of the audience, stone-faced*) Then in one week we lost all four of them. The first to go was my little 4-month-old baby, Liam. Two days later, 3-year-old Elizabeth. The next day, 2-year-old Terence. Three days later, I laid out my eldest, Catherine, 5 years old. (*A long pause. Then, softly*) The first shall be the last and the last shall be the first. (*A deep breath*) But, like Job, the Lord was not yet through with me. The day after we buried Catherine, George dragged himself home from work, took to his bed and died peacefully in his sleep. He was 37.

What does a woman do after the earth suddenly opens up and swallows her? Well, I guess you do what I did. You do your burying. You do your crying. You do your feeling sorry for yourself. Then you wipe your eyes, blow your nose and get on with it. I sold everything I owned and went to Chicago. (*She crosses to the hotel room and steps into it*) I sat in a dingy hotel room for three days, sorting out my options, trying to come to some decisions about what to do, trying not to think about Memphis. I finally decided. I was a very good seamstress, so I made the decision to open up a dressmaking shop. In six months I had more business than I could handle. Many of my customers were society page women, like the mayor's wife and Mrs. George Pullman—he made those railroad sleeping cars, you know. A real son of a bitch. And she wasn't very far behind. But they spent good money, so what the hell. In four years I'd prospered to the point of taking in a

partner. Then came October eighth, 1871. That date ring a
bell with anyone? Well, I'll tell you, it rang *my* bell. October eighth, 1871, was the date of the Great Chicago Fire.
And, along with thousands of others, it wiped me out.
Clean as a goddamned hound's tooth.

One night I was just walking around in a neighborhood
near where I lived when I stumbled into a union organizing meeting in an old abandoned church. One thing led to
another, and before the night was over I had talked myself
into a job as an organizer.

Now, to understand what union organizers were up
against, you have to understand the abuses that went on,
the criminal neglect that existed in the operation of coal
mines and factories and other industries. There were virtually no federal or state laws on industrial safety. Those
that were on the books were simply ignored by both industry and government. The consequence was that human life
wasn't worth a damn, especially in the coal mines. Now, to
some people that might sound like an overly dramatic
thing to say. But it doesn't begin to match the cold, hard
facts.

In 1871, one hundred-twelve miners lost their lives, and
another three hundred thirty-one were horribly injured in
one Pennsylvania county. Thirty-six years later, when
enough time had gone by to allow for some improvements
in mine safety, the slaughter was still going on. In West
Virginia—now listen to this—three hundred sixty-one
miners were wiped off the face of the earth in simultaneous explosions in two mines owned by the same company,
mines that were supposed to be models of safety. According to the company! And in that same month another three
hundred forty-one miners were killed in four other mine
explosions in various parts of the country. We're talking

here a total of *seven hundred-two* miners killed at work in *one* month! One *month!* And the attitude of the mine owners and factory owners was absolutely barbarous! Safety precautions were too expensive, they said. The accidents were mostly the fault of the stupid workers, they said. Hogwash! There was one incident I know of where a miner drove his mule cart into the mine for another load of coal and part of the overhead came crashing down on him. The mine owner rushed to the scene and the first thing he asked was whether the mule had been killed. You see, the mule cost one hundred-twenty dollars. The miner cost nothing, not even compensation to his widow.

I've organized workers in a lot of different industries in a lot of different states: women beer-bottle washers in Milwaukee, steel workers and railroad workers in Pennsylvania, factory workers in Illinois, farm workers in California, mill workers in Alabama and Georgia. But I guess the one group I felt the deepest for was the coal miners. Coal mining is the most fiercesomely dangerous industry in the world. And the people who own the mines and run them are the biggest bastards in the world. Of course, they returned the compliment. They had newspapers print all kinds of stories about me. One paper called me a "vulgar, heartless creature," and accused me of having been a prostitute before going to work for the union. Well, if I was a prostitute the profession must have been in one helluva shape!

The only place in the country that could match West Virginia in the brutal treatment of coal miners was Colorado. In both states it was a conspiracy among the state government, the mine owners and the military. And it had been going on for years. As a matter of fact, the first time I was in Colorado was a number of years ago when the UMW sent me there to investigate conditions in the coal camps, where the miners lived. I disguised myself as an itinerant peddler and walked through the coal fields and saw for myself the miserable conditions imposed on the miners and their families. Ten years went by before I returned to Trinidad, and things hadn't changed. In fact, they'd gotten worse. A strike was in progress. A violent strike, and the miners were getting the worst of it. The UMW sent me in to try to turn things around. Ten minutes after I checked into my hotel room in Trinidad, there was a knock on my door. It was General John Chase, head of the state militia that was now stationed in Trinidad. He didn't mince words. "Get the hell out of Trinidad right now," he said, "or you go to jail!" (*She turns as if facing him*) I said, "Nothing doing, General! This is one person you don't push around!" I said. "This is a free country and I've got a right to go where I damn please!" (*She turns back to the audience*) Well, they marched me to a nearby hospital, popped me into a room, placed five guards over me on a twenty-four-hour watch and denied me contact with the newspaper reporters or anyone else.

A committee of miners' wives decided that they would stage a protest march to get me released. They got a city parade permit and rounded up more than one thousand women and children, no men, to parade through the streets of Trinidad. They carried numerous signs and banners calling for the release of Mother Jones.

The parade had barely gotten underway when General Chase and a company of cavalry blocked the street with their horses. The general ordered the marchers to disperse. They refused. Somehow the general's horse became skittish and reared up, throwing the general to the ground. The women started laughing, of course. The general became furious. He yelled to his troops, "Clear those women off the street!" (*She reaches into a pocket of her dress, pulls*

out a folded newspaper clipping and unfolds it) Let me
read you a newspaper clipping that described what happened. (*She reads aloud*) "Spurs sank home and the cavalry mounts plunged forward with snorts. Sabers flashed in
the bright sunlight. Laughter at General Chase's accident
turned to screams of terror. The women began to run back.
Mrs. Maggie Hammons was slashed across the forehead
with a saber; Mrs. George Gibson's ear was almost severed
from her head. Mrs. Thomas Braley threw up her hands in
front of her face and they were slashed by a sword.

"A cavalryman leaned from his horse and struck Mrs.
James Lanigan with the flat of his saber, knocking her to
the ground. Another soldier leaned down and smashed 10-
year-old Robert Arguello in the face with his fist. The
paraders turned and ran. Mrs. R. Verna, who had been
carrying the American flag, was pursued by a cavalryman
who tore the flag from her grasp and knocked her down
with his horse. General Chase, mounted again, was yelling
like a madman. A thousand women and children scurried
for safety." (*She silently folds the clipping and returns it to
her pocket*) This was Trinidad, Colorado, the United States
of America in the twentieth century. Even after a report
was issued by a special state commission months later,
condemning this piece of savagery, it was a long time
before Colorado corrected its abusive treatment of coal
miners and rejoined the human race.

I was born in Ireland a good many years ago. My family
moved to Canada when I was a child. I attended a Catholic
school in Toronto, going on to high school and afterward to
a convent college where I obtained a teaching certificate.
Then I left home. And that was the last time I ever saw my
parents or contacted them in any way. (*Short pause*) And if
you're wondering what happened between us—it's none
of your business.

I crossed the border into Michigan and taught for a while in a Catholic school, but I was appalled at the heavy-handed discipline the sisters dished out, so I quit.

As I mentioned a little earlier, although I worked with all kinds of labor groups, I spent more time with coal miners than with any other group. They were *my* boys.

I was sent to Norton, Virginia, one hot summer to prop up some striking miners. Their strike wasn't going well at all. They were getting beat up by vicious mine guards, their money was giving out and they were about ready to give up. There I was, this little old woman in a black dress and black hat, standing on top of a wagon in the middle of an open field, talking to about five hundred miners. (*She assumes the persona of Mother Jones, union organizer, a tough cookie, a powerful speaker*) "Your president introduced me by saying I was going to give you some good words of advice. Well, he was wrong! I didn't come here to give advice! I came here to raise hell! I came here to tell you whiney sissyboys that if you keep letting yourselves get pushed around, then you ought to go on home, diaper your kids and let your *women* run this strike! Now, I know you've had some hard times in this strike, but you listen to me! I don't subscribe to violence, but, godammit, when peaceful strikers like you fellahs get your heads broken and your teeth bashed out by those bloodthirsty goons hired by the mine owners, then I say it's time to stand up on your hind legs and fight back! I say to you men it's time to stop turning the other cheek! It's time to stop backing away! (*She pauses, scanning the faces in front of her. Then she resumes in a deliberate pace but building*) It's time you men here in Virginia show the owners that you believe enough in what you're striking for to *fight* for it, if you're forced to! Let me tell you, I've been in jail more times than you can count, and I expect to go again. But if you're too

cowardly to fight back, *I* will fight! *I* will stand up to those
goons if you won't! *I* will kick 'em where it hurts if you
won't! (*She is breathing hard. A brief pause*) You ought to
be ashamed of yourselves, actually to the Lord you ought,
just to see one old woman who is not afraid of those blood-
hounds, by God! One old woman who is ready and willing
to stand up and spit right in their eye—while all of you
stand around, waiting for a miracle to happen!" (*She stands
there, defiant, breathing heavily, staring at her audience.
Then she abruptly drops the role, steps down from the
platform and stands there. Then, in a conversational tone*)
As I remember, I was seventy-four when I had that little
chat.

One thing about being the only woman organizer in the
country, I shuttled around from one state to the other, one
city to the next. I was always on the go, just like Johnny
Appleseed. Only instead of planting seeds I planted ideas.
I also got a lot of people mad at me, especially industrialists, big business people. There were a few labor officials
who didn't much care for me, either. They thought I was
too independent, which I was, I guess. A number of judges
couldn't abide the sight of me because I wouldn't kowtow
to them. They sent me to jail time after time for what they
called inciting workers to violence. But that was their way
of playing footsies with the mine owners and other industrialists.

Over half the judges in this country don't understand or
know anything about law, in my opinion. If Jesus Christ
were to go before old Judge Claude Malone out in Arizona
and tell him he was breaking the Ten Commandments by
his actions, Malone would tell Jesus that the Ten Commandments are unconstitutional in this country. The trouble with Malone is he's been dead for forty years but
doesn't know it.

President Taft once invited me to the White House to talk about labor problems. We talked for almost an hour. Now, I knew he belonged to the Wall Street crowd, but he showed his hand. He was honest about it. But that other fellah, Teddy the Monkey Chaser, when he was president he talked out of both sides of his mouth at the same time. His way of settling labor disputes was to use the militia and bayonets. (*She crosses to the hotel room and enters*) I was down in southern Arizona in the early 1900s, a dusty little town named Douglas, right on the Mexican border. There was a copper mine nearby and I was doing some organizing among the miners. I was in my hotel room one night getting ready to go to bed. It was about ten-thirty or so. I was about to pull down the window shade . . . (*she simulates looking out of a window*) . . . when I saw a big touring car pull up in front of the newspaper office across the street. What attracted my attention was the way the car skidded to a stop. I saw two men get out and hurry into the newspaper office. In no time they came out, holding a struggling young man between them. Following them was an older man who was yelling and waving his arms. The two men shoved the younger man into the car, got in themselves and away the car went. The older man just stood there, shaking his head. (*She simulates pulling down the window shade*) Well, I thought it was just some kind of a fracas that wasn't unusual in small border towns like Douglas, and went ahead getting ready for bed. In about five minutes there was a knock at my door. It turned out to be the editor of the Spanish language newspaper in Douglas, the man I'd seen yelling and waving his arms. And what I'd seen through my window, I learned, was not some local to-do, but a kidnapping. Not by a bunch of gangsters, but by some agents of the Porfirio Diaz government in Mexico. (*Pause, looking straight at one of the audience in the first row*) Well, I didn't know about Porfirio Diaz, either, so you don't need to feel stupid. Pablo—

Pablo Rios, the newspaper editor—filled me in. (*Now to the rest of the audience*) Diaz, you see, was the head of the Mexican government, but he was more than just the president. He was a dictator, the most vicious, arrogant dictator in Mexico's history. He'd been in office for *thirty-one* years! Can you imagine? He was supported by the wealthy landowners who saw to it that the ballot boxes were stuffed every election—in favor of Diaz. He thought he *owned* Mexico, that he could do whatever the hell he wanted to do.

The working class—the laborers, the farmers, the factory workers—got the short end of the stick, of course. The young man who was kidnapped was named Manuel Sarabia. He was one of the leaders who opposed Diaz and, consequently, was on the Diaz death list to be shot on sight. When things got too hot for Sarabia he ducked across the border into Douglas and got a job on Pablo Rios' newspaper.

What really got my goat, what really upset me, was the way those Mexican thugs just barged into Douglas, across the United States border, in full view of witnesses, and grabbed young Sarabia. (*She sits on the edge of the bed as if facing Rios*) I finally got around to asking Rios why he hadn't gone to the local authorities instead of coming to me.

"Because they won't do anything," he said.

I asked him what he expected me to do.

"Arouse public opinion in this country," he answered. "Force Diaz to release Sarabia."

I told him I wasn't a magician, that I couldn't pull rabbits out of a hat.

"But you have influence," he said. "You have respect."

I wasn't at all sure that I should get mixed up in an international situation like that. But Rios pointed out that the people being hurt by all this were the poor and the working class Mexicans, the little people, the kind of people I fought for in the United States. I saw his point.

About midnight we woke up Whitey Gossett, president of the copper miners union. He answered the door in his long johns, real grumpy, and wanted to know what the hell I was doing knocking on his door at that hour. I said, "It's not dignified to hold a conversation in your underwear, Whitey. Go put on some clothes. We need to talk."

Well, I explained the situation to him and he agreed to call an emergency meeting of the union the next night so that I could talk to them. There were six hundred forty men in union hall the next night when I got up to speak.

I told them about the kidnapping of Manuel Sarabia by Mexican agents who had crossed the border illegally. I told them who Sarabia was and that American workers should do what they could to help Mexican workers. (*Now she is in the middle of a highly charged speech*) ". . . and I tell you that this kidnapping is a criminal act, not only against Manuel Sarabia, one of Mexico's great young patriots, but against every person in the United States who believes in freedom! It is a criminal act against you and against me! I am outraged! I am incensed that Porfirio Diaz, this bloodthirsty pirate on a throne, this pissant of a dictator, has the gall to think he can reach across the border and stomp the Constitution of the United States under his muddy boots! We have to help our brothers in Mexico. We can't turn our backs on them. And I'll tell you how we can help. We can protest to every one of our elected officials. In Douglas! In the statehouse! In Washington! Right up to Teddy Roosevelt himself! And we can try to get our friends and relatives wherever they are in the country to do the same thing! (*Short pause*) Are you willing to spend a few dollars of your own money to send a telegram to the White House? Let me see a show of hands. (*She scans the audience, then smiles*) I'm proud of you!"

Well, we really rolled old Teddy out of bed that night. (*She chuckles*) I learned later that thousands of telegrams hit the White House. Major newspapers across the country featured the Sarabia kidnapping on the front page. And you can bet that that kind of publicity wasn't an accident, if you know what I mean. (*She winks*) The result was that Roosevelt called in the Mexican ambassador and gave him hell. Told him that if Sarabia wasn't released immediately, Mexico would find itself in more trouble than it could handle. Eight days after Sarabia was kidnapped, he was delivered to the border at Douglas and set free.

Heavy-handedness doesn't always do what you'd like for it to do, but it has its place. I've been accused of overusing it, but I only employ the tactic when I think it's necessary. I've often gone in the other direction. I remember an incident in Arnot, Pennsylvania. This one had a little humor in it.

The coal company had turned down a request by the miners for a wage increase. So the miners went on strike. The trouble was that the strike didn't shut down the mines because the operators had gone out and hired a bunch of scabs to come in and replace the strikers. Winter was setting in and the mines were going full blast. The only thing the strikers could do was to stand out in the cold with their picket signs and watch the scabs go into the mines in the morning and stream out in the evening. I was sent to Arnot to see if I could get the company to reopen wage negotiations and settle the strike. (*She crosses to the hotel room and enters*) I checked into the only hotel in Arnot and began a series of meetings with the strike leaders. (*She sits on the bed, facing the audience*) After a few minutes of talking I could see that they were licked, discouraged. And for good reason. Not one of them could pull even a one-dollar bill out of his pocket. They couldn't buy food for their families, couldn't buy medicine or clothing. The only thing that kept them going was the help of sympathetic townspeople, who provided food and a few other necessities. I went to the superintendent of the coal company and asked for a meeting. He laughed. So far as he was concerned he was sitting in the catbird seat. As long as he had scabs working the mines, he didn't have to meet with me or anyone else. My problem, then, was to find a way to get rid of the scabs. (*She leaves the hotel room*) I came up with an idea. I got together with all the wives of the strikers and explained my plan. When I finished, they all burst out laughing. You'd have thought we were planning a Christmas party instead of a scab-busting party. Late the next afternoon I had about a hundred women standing outside the mouth of the main mine. Each of them was carrying a pot or a frying pan in one hand and a hammer or big kitchen spoon in the other. I stood off to one side, a number of yards away. At five o'clock the quitting whistle blew and the women got ready. In a short while the scabs began streaming out of the mine, each one leading his mule. As planned, the women waited until most of the scabs and mules were out in the open. Then, with a lot of screaming and whooping and hollering, the women charged the scabs, beating on their pots and pans right in the ears of the mules. I tell you if anyone was interested in what bedlam sounded like, this was it. The mules, of course, were frightened by the noise and began rearing up and braying and kicking, dragging the scabs along after them through the mud and puddles of mine water, all the while pursued by the women. Well, inside of two minutes all you could see was the mules galloping down the hillside with the scabs chasing after them. (*She chuckles as she crosses back to the hotel room. She sits down at the desk, takes out a sheet of paper from the drawer and begins writing with a pencil. As she writes, her voice is heard on the speaker system*) ". . . and I'm happy to report to you, Jim, that, mainly as the result of the Women's Brigade, as I call them, the company has been unable to hire another scab to work the mines. My women just scared the holy hell out of them. Consequently, we were able to settle the strike forty-eight hours later and get all of our men back to work. With a wage increase. Now, if you don't mind, Jim, I'd like to take a couple of weeks off. There's a child labor situation down in Alabama I'd like to check on. On my own time, of course. Regards to everyone at headquarters. Mother Jones." (*She folds the letter, slips it into an envelope which she licks and seals, placing the envelope on the desk. She stands and walks out of the room*) Several months earlier I was down in Alabama, organizing some of the miners in the area. While I was there, the boys and I were chewing the fat one evening and they told me about labor abuses in the textile mills just outside Birmingham that they said made some of the coal mine problems look like a tea party. I asked what kind of abuses and they said child labor abuses. They went on to describe conditions that were so inhuman that I found it hard to believe them. I was very familiar, of course, with the barbaric child labor practices of the coal industry, but I'd never had a chance to really explore the situation in the textile mills. What I found when I went down there appalled me. I've seen a lot of terrible things in my time, but nothing prepared me for what I found in Alabama.

I got a room in the cheapest hotel in town. The first thing I did was to exchange my regular outfit for a gingham dress, an old sunbonnet and a beat up cardigan sweater with holes in the elbows. Then I went out to one of the mills and applied for a job. The manager looked me up and down and said, "You're pretty old to be looking for a job, aren't you?" I looked him straight in the eye and told him I could outwork *him* any day in the week. He laughed and then said that it was the policy of the mill not to hire anyone unless they had some children that could be hired at the same time. When I asked him how old the children had to be, he said that they hired them from 6 on up. Well, I gave him a cock-and-bull story that I had four young grandchildren staying with a friend in Knoxville while I looked for a job. Their ma was dead, I told him, and I was taking care of them. I said that I could have them in Birmingham in a few days. So he hired me, with the provision that I bring the kids in as soon as they arrived. I asked what the pay was. He said it was the same as every place else: forty cents a day, fourteen hours a day for me; ten cents a day, twelve hours for the kids.

I started work the next day at one of the looms. Now, I had read the book *Oliver Twist* by that English writer, Charles Dickens, that told how cruel the children were treated in the English factories and mills. But let me tell you, what I saw in that mill matched the very worst conditions that Mr. Dickens described in his book.

The mill actually was a huge, long shed containing maybe ninety, ninety-five or so looms. I estimated that there were at least two hundred people working at various jobs. The noise was horrendous, nerve-wracking: the whirring of the big wheels and the pounding and clacking of looms and related machinery. People had to shout to be heard. One thing that struck me was that there seemed to be more children working than adults. What with the loom wheels and the flywheels of the machinery and the endless belts flapping at high speed, none with protective shielding, the children were constantly at risk. It was just criminal.

I saw young boys and girls with missing fingers, many with blood-stained bandages wrapped around a finger or hand. Work started at five in the morning. At around eight o'clock that first morning, I noticed a boy no more than seven had crawled off to a corner and was curled up, fast asleep. You could see that he was exhausted, poor thing. One of the supervisors spotted him. Without a word, the supervisor walked over to a large metal container of water, got a dipperful of the cold water, walked back to the sleeping child and dashed the water in his face. The startled boy jerked awake, wild-eyed with fear. When he saw the supervisor he jumped to his feet and ran back to his job. The supervisor followed him and kicked the boy, knocking him to the floor. I tell you I had trouble keeping myself from going to that supervisor and giving him a piece of my mind. But I didn't.

At the lunch break I saw the boy and a beautiful little girl with long, blond hair sitting with a young woman who was obviously their mother. I sat next to her and as we ate our sandwiches we got to talking. I learned that the little boy's name was Chuckie and his sister's name was Sissy. The boy was not quite 7, she was 8.

I asked the mother if she wasn't afraid that the children would get hurt working in the mill. She said she was scared to death from the minute they started until quitting time.

"Then why do you let them do it?" I asked.

She looked at me as if I didn't have good sense and said, "You ever try to feed a family of three young'uns and a husband stove up in the mines for less than three dollars a week? We need the money. That's why they work."

Then I said to her, "You ever think about joining a union?"

I thought for a minute she was going to have conniption fits. She looked around to see if anyone had overheard me. Then she lowered her voice almost to a whisper. "You crazy?" she said. "Boss hear that word around here and you're fired. Then where'd you be? Who'll buy your food? Who'll pay the rent? The union? Like hell they will!" Just then the work bell started ringing and that ended that.

About a week later the manager came up to my loom and pulled me aside. "Where the hell are your grandchildren?" he said. "They should have been here by now."

Before I could answer, there was a piercing, blood-chilling scream from one of the children. This was followed by a series of shrieks, a woman's shrieks, and she wouldn't quit, just kept on shrieking. People began running past us toward the back of the building. Somebody must have thrown the switch because the machinery began grinding to a stop. The manager and I both started running toward the back where a big cluster of workers had gathered. With the machinery off, you could now hear moaning and wailing coming from the center of the cluster. I pushed my way into the crowd and saw Sissy's mother sitting on the floor, holding Sissy in her arms. Both were drenched in blood. The mother just sat there, cradling that little girl and rocking back and forth. (*She is horror-stricken, her voice almost failing*) Then I saw that Sissy's long blond hair wasn't where it was supposed to be. It had been pulled off her head. And it wasn't blond anymore. It was blood red. So were her head and face. Her hair had been caught in one of the flywheels and she had been scalped. (*She kneels down*) I knelt down and put my arm around the mother, trying to comfort her. Then I yelled at the manager, "Can't we get a doctor in here, for God's sake?" He just looked at me.

"What for?" he said. "She's dead, ain't she? Just get the two of 'em out of here so everybody can get back to work."

I got to my feet and flew at that man. I was in a rage. I was furious. And I was crying. I pushed my face up close to his and screamed, "You son of a bitch! You lousy son of a bitch!" Then I hauled back and slapped him as hard as I could. (*She whips her open hand through the air*) I ran out of that building, tears streaming down my face. I hadn't cried like that since I buried my own four little ones and George. (*She brushes away the tears as she crosses into the hotel room. She sits at the desk, takes a sheet of paper from the drawer, takes up the pencil and starts writing. As she does, her voice is heard on the speaker system*) "Dear Jim. After two weeks at this mill I can flatly say that this is the most dreadful, the most blatant exploitation of children and the worst abuse of child labor laws I have ever encountered. I have watched tiny little children endangering life and limb all day long. It has upset me so badly that I haven't been able to eat. I haven't been able to sleep. Today I saw a beautiful little girl killed while she worked in all that machinery. Even as I write I can't get the horrible picture out of my mind. I pray that God damn to eternal hell the northern capitalists who own these mills. Jim, I have made up my mind to go north again to continue the fight I have lost here in Birmingham. I won't be coming back to the United Mine Workers for a while. I hate to leave you in the lurch, but this is something I must do. I know you'll understand. Mother Jones."

(She folds the sheet, puts it into an envelope, addresses the envelope and leaves it on the desk. She stands, walks out of the hotel room and exits. Blackout.)

Mother Jones enters and hesitates a moment before speaking.

MOTHER JONES: I was a long time getting over Birmingham. I first went back to Chicago to see if I could renew old friendships, to get away from labor matters for a while. It was hard to do. *Mother* Jones kept getting in the way of the *Mary* Jones I used to be. Too many years had gone by. Too many things had happened. After a week or so I knew I had made a mistake. You can't go backward in time. But it wasn't just that. I kept hearing that one, shattering scream of little Sissy's, and I knew I had to do something about it. Now. The *Chicago Tribune* helped make up my mind.

The *Tribune* printed a story about a massive strike of textile workers in Philadelphia. One hundred thousand workers had left their jobs at six hundred mills in the Philadelphia area. *Sixteen* thousand of the workers were children, many of them under the legal age of 13. The basis of the strike was a demand by the workers for a reduction in the work week from sixty hours to fifty-five hours. What interested me, however, was the situation with the children. The story pointed out that Pennsylvania law prohibited the employment of children under the age of 13, which meant that most of the sixteen thousand children strikers had been illegally employed by the various mills. Here was something I could sink my teeth into. I took the next train for Philadelphia.

When I got there I went directly to the textile workers union headquarters and introduced myself to the business agent, a youngish man by the name of Lonnie Bostock. He barely had time to greet me. He was like one of the Christians being held at bay by the lions. The place was swamped by strikers, many of them still holding picket signs. Off to one side was a group of young children. One look told me they were mill workers. They had all the telltale signs I'd become familiar with in Birmingham. Several youngsters were missing a thumb, several others with fingers off at the knuckles, a number of them wearing still-bloody bandages around their hands, a few of them missing a hand, many of them round-shouldered from carrying heavy rolls of yarn. Most of them couldn't have been more than 10–11 years old.

After about a half-hour, Bostock managed to clear the office and we had a chance to talk. I told him about my experience in Birmingham, and he just shook his head. The textile industry was the same all over, he said, not just in Alabama and Pennsylvania. I asked him if he had tried to get the local newspapers to run stories about how unsafe the mills were, and how they were violating state child labor laws.

He had indeed tried, he said, but the papers wouldn't print the stories. Why not, I asked him.

"Simple," he said. "The mill owners are big stockholders in both newspapers. They had the stories killed."

I said, "Well, the mill owners may have stock in the newspapers, but, by God, I have stock in these children and I'm not about to see that stock go down the drain."

Bostock asked me what I planned to do. "I don't know, yet," I told him. "Let me sleep on it. I'll see you in the morning."

I went back to my hotel to have supper. On my way into the dining room I bought a newspaper to read while I ate.

I sat down at my table and looked at the newspaper. Right on the front page was the answer to what I was going to do about those children. I folded the paper, had my supper, went up to my room and had a good night's sleep.

Bright and early the next morning I was back at union headquarters. "Lonnie," I said, "I've got my plan all worked out about those children. I'm going to arrange a little publicity," I told him. "I'm going to arrange something that'll have every big-city newspaper on the Eastern seaboard chasing after us for stories about those kids."

That got his attention. I told him that a story in last night's newspaper had given me the idea. The story reported that President Theodore Roosevelt and his family had taken up residence in their summer home at Oyster Bay on Long Island, some one hundred twenty-five miles from Philadelphia. My plan was to stage a children's march from Philadelphia to Oyster Bay to try to persuade the President to support stronger child labor laws. We would be tramping through all the towns and cities between Philadelphia and New York City. Hundreds of thousands of people would read about and see the marchers. On top of that, we would hold mass meetings and explain to the people why we were making the march. In no time we would be the talk of the country, and so would child labor laws.

Bostock asked if I planned to participate in the march, myself. I said I sure as hell was. "That's a pretty long hike for a woman in her mid-70s," he said.

I told him he sounded like the man who had hired me in Birmingham. Well, the long and short of it was that Bostock agreed to help me put the march together. He called a meeting of several hundred parents of the children and

introduced me. Fortunately, I didn't really need the introduction. Everyone there knew who Mother Jones was, and
many of them waved to me and called out nice things to
me. The main thing was that they trusted me, and in less
than an hour I had gotten their approval for the march.

In one week we were ready. Three hundred children and
their parents and four horse-drawn covered wagons made
up the march. Most of the children had little knapsacks on
their backs and carried signs and banners.

Just as we were about to move out, a little boy—he looked
to be about eight or nine—came up to me. He had the
stooped, round-shouldered posture of a mill boy. He said
he had to talk to me. He looked very serious. I asked him
what he wanted to talk to me about.

"Well," he said, "My ma said I oughtta ride in one of the
wagons 'sted of marchin' 'cause I'm so little. But I can
march good as anybody. Ma says she'll leave it up to you."

I managed to keep a straight face. I bent down to be more
on his level, and asked him what his name was. Jimmy, he
said. Jimmy Ashworth. I asked him how old he was. He
said, "Ten. But I'm little for my age."

I asked him what he did in the mills and he told me he
carried rolls of yarn from the stacks to the looms. I
straightened up and said, "Well, Jimmy, we don't want to
go against your ma's wishes, do we? But I'll tell you what
let's do. Tell her it's fine with me if you want to march with
the rest of the children, provided," and I held up my
forefinger, "provided you ride a while in the wagon whenever she tells you. All right?"

Jimmy was all smiles. He said, "Yes, *ma'am!* Thanks, Mother Jones!" and he was off running. I turned to Lonnie Bostock and asked him how much one of those rolls weighed. He told me they averaged about thirty, thirty-five pounds. I watched little undersize Jimmy running back to tell his mother the good news. Ten years old, small for his age, carrying virtually every day of his life a burden that should have been borne by a grown man. I knew then what I would call this march: The Children's Crusade.

I've had some memorable experiences in my lifetime, but the Children's Crusade is one that I'll never forget. We were on the road a little more than three weeks, almost the full month of July. We marched through dust and heat, through summer thunderstorms, through one town and city after another: Bristol, Morrisville, Trenton, New Brunswick, Elizabeth, Hoboken. And in each town we were greeted like conquering heroes. People jammed the sidewalks and streets, cheering us, encouraging us, bringing us food and drink when we stopped at noon or in some field for the night.

And how did all these people know who we were and when we were coming to their town or city? By the headlines and stories in newspapers all over the East. And what pleased me the most was that the Children's Crusade was generating exactly the kind of response I had hoped for.

We were camped for the night in a field just outside Princeton, New Jersey, on our final leg to New York. It was still daylight and I was sitting on a camp stool, soaking my feet in a pan of water and chatting with some of the parents, when a well-dressed man wearing a Vandyke beard and skimmer straw hat approached us. He apologized for interrupting us and said he was looking for

Mother Jones. I told him he had found her, bare feet and all, and asked what I could do for him.

He introduced himself as Professor Arthur Holzworth, Chairman of the Economics Department at Princeton University. He was there, he said, to invite me to lecture before a combined seminar of all the economic students and faculty members of the department.

I was too tired to be giving lectures and was about to tell him so when it occurred to me that here was a marvelous opportunity. So I accepted the invitation. He was to pick me up in the morning in time for a nine o'clock seminar. I was waiting for him the next morning, and waiting with me was little Jimmy Ashworth who I was going to have sitting on the platform with me. Professor Holzworth showed up promptly at nine and the three of us made the ten-minute walk to the campus together. (*She steps up on the center platform and stands facing the audience*) The room where I was to lecture was a large amphitheatre, and it was packed. Professor Holzworth called the seminar to order and began his introduction of me. I was sitting off to one side with Jimmy. The introduction was the usual folderol. He called me one of the country's most remarkable women, the first female labor organizer in the United States, a former teacher and said he considered me a walking textbook on the economic impact of labor unrest. I walked to the center of the platform, adjusted my glasses and faced the audience, taking my time before beginning. (*She slowly scans the audience, then begins, her voice resonant*) "What I'm going to tell you may make some of you uncomfortable, but there's nothing I can do about that. You are going to hear some ugly truths, and one of those truths is that the nation's industrialists are crucifying little children for the sake of the almighty dollar.

"Fifty years ago there was a cry against slavery, and men gave up their lives to stop the selling of black children on the auction block. Today the *white* child is sold for a pittance to the manufacturer—C.O.D.—and not a hand is raised, not a voice speaks out against this vile abuse of human morality!

"The process begins by paying totally unrealistic and inadequate wages to the *parents* of the children. Because money is needed to buy necessities, parents allow their little underage children to work in the mills and the mines, even though they know—and the industrialists know—that in Pennsylvania and some other states it is against the law to employ children under the age of 13.

"We are making this march, these little ones, their parents and I, hoping to touch the heart and the intellect of President Roosevelt. (*Now her voice takes on an edge*) By embarking on this Children's Crusade, for that's what it really is, a crusade, we have brought out of the closet the skeleton hidden there by the industrialists, and we have *rattled* that skeleton in the face of the American people! (*She lowers the intensity*) Professor Holzworth has called me a walking textbook in certain aspects of economics. But, now, I want to introduce you to the *real* textbook in economics. (*She turns and walks back to the platform where Jimmy Ashworth is sitting. She puts one arm around his shoulder, then goes back center, her arm still around his shoulder*) This is Jimmy Ashworth. Jimmy knows what I'm going to say, and he's not going to be embarrassed about it. (*Pause*) But I hope *you will* be! (*Pause*)

"Jimmy is 10 years old. He is stooped over because his spine is curved from the burden of carrying, day after day, bundles of yarn that weigh thirty-five pounds! He works in a carpet factory in Philadelphia, ten hours a day, six days a week at a pay of three dollars a week, never getting a chance to go to school, while the children of the rich (*Pause, her eyes a narrow gleam*) while the children of the rich, whose Philadelphia mansions were built on the bent backs and broken bones of *thousands* of Jimmy Ashworths! While the children of the rich (*slowly, deliberately*) are getting their higher education!" (*She holds for a few seconds, her face and her whole body expressing defiance. Then she drops the role and steps down*)

From Princeton we went straight on into New York City where we camped out in Central Park, children, parents, horses, wagons and all. I don't think New Yorkers had ever seen anything like the spectacle we presented, because we were the object of a lot of sightseeing. The place also was swarming with reporters, not just from New York but from all over the country, one even from London. One of them told me that he had it on good authority that the President was not going to see me or any of the children because we were too much of a political hot potato. I said, well, it didn't make too much difference one way or the other any more. We'd already made our point with the people of the country and they had made no bones about the way they felt. They were all for us. That made Teddy strictly second fiddle, so far as I was concerned. But I would try to see him, anyway.

First I wanted to give the children a treat after their long journey. I made arrangements to transport the whole kit and kaboodle to Coney Island for a day at the beach. Most of the children had never seen the ocean before and they were simply entranced. Little Jimmy Ashworth just stood, wide-eyed, at the water's edge, watching the waves roll in.

"It just keeps flushing and flushing," he said in wonderment. (*She smiles in remembrance*)

The next day I was visited by two men from the Secret Service, and they made it official. The President sent his regrets but he would not be able to see us. I had the last word on that subject, however. I immediately called all the newspapers in the city and gave them the story. They played it for all it was worth. One headline said, "TEDDY HIDES FROM MOTHER!" I loved it. I don't know about Teddy.

There was one more thing I wanted to do for the children before we sent them back to Philadelphia. I wanted to stage a parade of all the children, their parents and the horses and wagons—right down the middle of New York City. I wanted the whole city to see these brave little boys and girls, and I wanted the children to experience a New York City ticker tape parade.

Now I knew that I'd have to get a permit to stage a parade in the city, but instead of going to the police I decided to go straight to the mayor. I always like to deal with the top man whenever I can, you know. Low, his name was. Mayor Seth Low. He didn't make me wait at all. Saw me right away. He was a tall kind of fellah, and real friendly, I thought. He invited me to sit down across the desk from him . . . (*she sits*) and told me how much he admired me for trying to help the children of the country. Then he asked me what he could do for me.

I told him I wanted a parade permit. "What kind of a parade?" he asked.

"For those children I brought from Philadelphia," I said. "I'd like to parade 'em down Madison Avenue," I said, "So New Yorkers can see what all the fuss is about."

Well, he harrumphed and cleared his throat and then said he was sorry but he couldn't give me a parade permit.

I said, "What do you mean you can't give me a parade permit? Why not?"

"Well, Mrs. Jones," he said, "neither you nor the children are citizens of New York City."

"What the hell's that got to do with it?" I said.

"Well," he said, "city ordinance requires that only citizens of the community qualify for parade permits."

"Is that your chief reason?" I asked. He said that it was.

"Well, Mr. Mayor," I said, "I think we can clear that up. I think we can straighten that out right now." Then I said, "You remember last summer when there was a parade down Madison Avenue for that piece of German royalty, Prince Henry? You remember that?" The mayor turned kind of red and allowed as how he did remember.

"And do you remember that the United States Congress voted forty-five thousand dollars to entertain him here in New York, and to fill his stomach?" I said. "And President Roosevelt hired a massage doctor to rub him down so he could get back to Germany in good shape?" I said. "You remember?" He just nodded his head.

"Was he a citizen of New York City, that German prince?" I said.

"No," the mayor said. "No, he wasn't."

"Did he create any wealth for this country?"

"Not that I know of," he said.

"Well," I said, "these children have. Don't they have the same right to parade as a foreign prince?"

Well, sir, the mayor slapped his hand down on his desk and said, "They sure do, by God! They sure do! I've been a jackass long enough!" he said. "I'll write you out a parade permit myself! Right now!" And he did, too. And he marched in the parade with me.

It was a wonderful parade. And a big one. Right down Madison Avenue, with marching bands from the police, the firemen and all kinds of other organizations. The crowds were enormous, lining both sides of the street, and they cheered and hollered and waved to us as we went by. (*She grins*) The children insisted that I lead the parade, and I tell you that was a real thrill. Even for an old geezer like me. There was another thrill that surpassed even that one. It came two months later. The Pennsylvania state legislature, the New York state legislature, the New Jersey state legislature and four other state legislatures passed legislation strengthening their child labor laws.

A newspaperman once asked me how I could live a life so full of confrontations; didn't it bother me? I told him, yes, sometimes it bothered the hell out of me. Sometimes I'd a lot rather be reading one of my favorite Robert Burns poems or thumbing through my Bible or enjoying some other little personal pleasure.

But I'd look around me, I said, and see so many mean sonsabitches pushing the little man around that I couldn't stand it. You know, I told him, the next generation will not condemn us for what we have *done;* they will charge and condemn us for what we have left *undone.* I believe that.

I've been accused of being irreligious because of some of the things I say, because I don't go to church. Well, let me straighten you out on that. First of all, I don't care what a person's religion is. Jew or Gentile, they're all the same to me. What gets my goat are the preachers. They stand up there on the pulpit every Sunday spouting all these platitudes about Jesus being there to look out for the meek and the mild in time of trouble.

Well, *Jesus* may be there, but where are the *preachers* when hard times come along? When the robber-baron coal mine operators throw miners and their families out of their company-owned shacks during strikes? I'll tell you where the preachers *aren't*. They aren't up there on the pulpit giving the mine owners hell or criticizing the use of trigger-happy mine guards, because the preachers know where the money is and they're afraid to offend the fat-cat operators. And that's the long and short of why I don't go to church.

Let's talk about West Virginia. Of all the time I've spent on union business—organizing locals, setting up contracts, working on strikes, helping miners and their families—the one place where I spent the most time was West Virginia. I know West Virginia like I know the back of my hand. There were sections of that state where union organizers didn't dare enter, for it was certain they would never leave alive. It was without question the hardest state to organize that I ever encountered.

The reason was that the state government gave the coal operators a free hand to do whatever they wanted to do. And what the operators did was to threaten reprisals if miners ever listened to union organizers. The consequence was that many miners resented any organizer showing up because of what the operators might do.

Many's the time I've rented a one-horse shay and driven up some of those mountain hollows where I knew maybe some thirty or forty miners lived. They were all non-union, of course, and I was going in there to see if I couldn't get them to join up. These were real wild sections, so I carried a big club, like a baseball bat, under the seat, just in case some smart-ass got out of hand or I met up with one of those goons hired by the mine owners. Never had to use the club, thank the good Lord. Generally, I was able to talk my way out of trouble spots. But it was common knowledge that any number of mine owners had threatened to kill me or shoot me. They said I ought to be run out of those mountains, that I ought to be shot on sight, locked up in an asylum. All kind of crazy things. Well, if they expected me to turn tail and run like a frightened rabbit, they had another thought coming.

The worst time I ever had in West Virginia was during the Paint Creek-Cabin Creek strike of 1912–1913. Paint Creek and Cabin Creek were coal camps near Charleston, the state capital, maybe fifteen, twenty miles away. The strike involved four thousand miners and more than thirty different coal companies.

It started in April, 1912, and by the time I got into it in November of that year, it had become one of the most violent battles in American history. The coal companies had hired almost a thousand mine guards, fully armed, including high-powered rifles and machine guns. On top of that, the state had sent in three companies of the National Guard—twenty-one hundred heavily armed soldiers. Martial law had been declared by Governor Glasscock, enabling the military to take complete control of the area.

When I got there, more than thirty miners had been killed, shot down by mine guards or National Guardsmen who, themselves, had also suffered some casualties. Without doubt, this was as close to civil war as anything I'd ever run into.

Winter had already struck in the mountains the day I arrived in Paint Creek. I stepped off the train and looked at the little wooden station sitting all by itself along the railroad tracks. Then I noticed three men in sheepskin coats walking toward me. They all carried rifles and had pistols strapped around their middle. I knew immediately what they were: coal company mine guards.

I put down my suitcase and waited for them to approach me. The biggest one came up to me and in a real arrogant manner asked if I were Mother Jones. I said I was, who wanted to know.

He said, "I do, by God! I'm Jim Coleman. Felts-Baldwin Detective Agency!"

I said, "Felts-Baldwin Goon Squad, you mean!"

Well, that made him really mad. He shook his finger in my face and said, "If you know what's good for you, old woman, you'll climb back on that train and get the hell out of here!"

I said to him, "Let me tell you something, young man. The only way you'll get me back on that train is to pick me up bodily and *put* me on it! And if you do, I'll be on the next train coming in!"

I just stood there, daring them to pick me up. The three of them looked at one another, not sure what they ought to do. Then I said, "Well, don't any of you big, brave men want the honor of manhandling an 83-year-old, defenseless woman?"

They just shuffled their feet, embarrassed-like. So I picked up my suitcase. "Then get the hell out of my way!" I said. "I have business to attend to!" And I pushed past them.

There were maybe fifty reporters covering the strike. One of them was a fellah named H.L. Mencken of the *Baltimore Sun*. He was what you'd call sharp-tongued, but I respected that because I had been accused of having the same affliction. One bitterly cold December morning, about a week before Christmas, I set out from Paint Creek to another coal camp called Mucklow, about a three-mile walk. I was scheduled to talk to a bunch of strikers who needed a little pumping up. Mencken asked if he could come along and do a little story on the meeting. I told him it could be dangerous, but he was welcome to come along if he wanted to.

The shortest way to Mucklow was to follow the railroad tracks which paralleled a pretty fast-moving creek, then cross a railroad trestle which spanned the creek.

We were walking along the tracks, talking, when I spotted one of the mine guards up ahead. As we got closer I recognized him. It was Jim Coleman. He was straddling the tracks, looking directly at us, holding his rifle at the ready. I warned Mencken that we could be walking into trouble and to keep his mouth shut, that I would do the talking.

When we were about twenty yards from Coleman he ordered us to stop, and asked where we were going. I told him I had a meeting in Mucklow and that Mr. Mencken was going with me at my invitation. Coleman asked how we planned to get into Mucklow. I said, across the railroad trestle yonder.

He said, "Oh, no you ain't, you old rabble-rouser. This is as far as you go." I told him I had as much right to use that trestle as anybody else.

"You got whatever right I tell you, old woman," he said. "But I tell you what I'm gonna do. Because I'm so big-hearted, I'm gonna let you go to Mucklow—if you wanna wade that creek to get there." And he grinned.

Well, Mencken's face was getting redder and redder. Finally, he couldn't contain himself any longer. "Now, wait a minute, you," he burst out. "Surely you're not going to force an 83-year-old woman to wade that ice cold creek?"

Coleman laughed. "She ain't gonna wade no creek," he said. "That old woman?"

I looked him in the eye for a few seconds, then I sat down on a boulder alongside the tracks and took off my shoes and stockings. I put them in my winter coat pockets, lifted up the hems of my dress and coat and walked out into the creek. Coleman's eyes about popped out of his head as I stepped into the cold water. Mencken had his pencil and notebook out, scribbling notes.

The creek was rocky and the water was moving fairly rapidly, but I was careful and got across without any trouble. When I reached the other side I called out to Mencken that I'd see him in Mucklow. Coleman just stood there, staring at me in disbelief. I heard him say, "Well, I'll be a son of a bitch!" I could see that Mencken had a big grin on his face.

"There *is* that possibility!" he said. (*She crosses to the courtroom and sits at the table*)

Two days before Christmas I was arrested by the National Guard and held for trial by a military court-martial, making me the first civilian ever tried by a court-martial in this country, outside of wartime. The trial was being held in complete secrecy—no newspapermen or any other civilians permitted to attend, except for the UMW lawyer and witnesses. And no information whatsoever about the trial released to the public. As soon as the trial opened, Cecil Watkins, the UMW lawyer, stood up.

"I would like to object to the court's decision to hold this trial in secret," he said. "You're not trying military personnel. You are attempting to try a civilian under military rules. That is illegal. At the very least, I feel that the newspaper reporters waiting outside this building should be admitted to the trial. How else will the public know what goes on here?"

Well, the court overruled him, of course, and the trial went on. They called witness after witness, mostly military people, trying to nail me to the wall. I refused to participate in the proceedings. I just sat there, watching them play out their little game, wondering how in God's name something like this could go on in the United States.

Finally, it was over and the three members of the court-martial left the room to consider their verdict. In less than ten minutes they were back with their decision: guilty on all four specifications, one of which was murder. Then the president of the court, Colonel Bollinger, rapped his gavel on the table and said that court stood adjourned until further notice. Cecil jumped to his feet.

"Just a minute, Colonel," he said. "This court says it finds Mrs. Jones guilty on all four specifications, but you say nothing about her sentence."

Bollinger told him that the sentence would be made known at an appropriate future date. Cecil exploded.

"But for God's sake, man!" he said. "How can you do that? What happens in the meantime? What happens to the defendant?"

Bollinger didn't bat an eye. The prisoner would be detained, he said. Where? Cecil asked. That's a matter of military security, Bollinger told him. I finally had all I could take. (*She stands, her hands planted on the table, leaning forward*) I looked straight at Colonel Bollinger. "You're talking about *me*, Colonel Bollinger," I said, "not military security! You're talking about my rights as an American citizen! Just who the hell do you think you are, you and your high and mighty court–martial?"

He just ignored me. He gathered up his papers and left the room, followed by the other officers of the court. (*She stands at the counsel table, looking down. Then she raises her head and walks slowly out of the courtroom and enters the hotel room*) That night I was placed in a closed touring car and driven to the little town of Pratt, not too far from Charleston. I was locked up in a small, cabin-like structure with only the bare necessities, and sat there for three long months. (*She sits on the end of the bed, facing the audience*) I learned later that not a soul, except the military and the governor, knew what had happened to me or where I was. Newspapers started running stories: Where is Mother Jones? The Strange Disappearance of Mother Jones, and so on.

Finally, a sympathetic young soldier helped me smuggle out a telegram to my good friend, United States Senator John W. Kern of Indiana. Four days later, there was a rattle at the door and in walked a young captain who had testified against me at the trial. Behind him was Cecil Watkins, a big smile on his face. (*She is standing now*) After Cecil and I had hugged each other, he told me that all hell had busted loose in the governor's office; that Senator Kern had read my telegram on the floor of the Senate and then called for a Senate investigation of the Paint Creek-Cabin Creek strike; that the newspapers had picked up on the story and were burning the hide off the state of West Virginia for keeping me secretly imprisoned for three months.

Am I free? I asked Cecil. You sure are, he said, by order of the governor himself. Then I asked him if he had ever found out what the court–martial had sentenced me to. It couldn't have been the three months they'd kept me in this little cabin.

When Cecil told me what the sentence was, I could hardly believe it. Twenty years in the West Virginia State Penitentiary! I started to laugh. Twenty years? At my age?

The captain came up to me, crooked his elbow and held it out to me. "Madam," he said, "we are going to Charleston. May I take your arm?"

I drew myself up and let him have it. "I am not a madam," I said. "I am Mother Jones! The government can't take my life and you can't take my arm!" (*A brief pause*) "But," I said, "you *can* take my suitcase!" With that I took Cecil's arm and walked out of that two-bit jailhouse.

I learned later that the governor had ordered the mine owners to sit down with the union and work out their differences. The result was a contract almost exactly like that we had been pushing for.

That was an experience that will live with me always. I will especially remember the inadvertent compliment the judge-advocate, the prosecutor, paid me during the trial. He pointed at me and said, "There sits the most dangerous woman in America! She comes into a state where peace and progress reign," he said, "she crooks her finger— twenty thousand men lay down their tools and walk out!" (*She smiles*) That's an overstatement, of course. The only people who have found me dangerous have been the robber-barons.

About two weeks after I was set free, I was invited to be the guest of honor at a mass meeting at Carnegie Hall in New York City. Although I hadn't fully recovered my strength, I decided I would accept the invitation because I had a few things I wanted to get off my chest, and Carnegie Hall would be a good place to do it.

I was met at Pennsylvania Station by reporters from the *New York Times*, the *Daily News*, the *New York Herald* and a bunch of others. They took my picture, interviewed me and followed me all the way to my hotel, where they took more pictures and asked more questions. I finally begged off and said I wanted to rest up a little before the big meeting that night.

Carnegie Hall was already filled to capacity when I got there with the reception committee. (*She crosses to the platform at Center, steps up on it and faces the audience*) A couple of other speakers preceded me, and then I was introduced. The audience rose to its feet and there was a lot of clapping and cheering and whistling, which finally quieted down and I began. (*She pauses a moment, then begins to speak in a quiet tone*)

"I have just come from a God-cursed country known as West Virginia; from a state which has produced some of our best and brightest statesmen; a state where conditions are too awful for your imagination. I shall tell you some things tonight that are awful to contemplate, but it is best you know of them.

"I saw men, women and children evicted from their homes in the dark of night; forced to live in flimsy tents in the middle of a bitter, cold winter. I saw miners shot down in cold blood in a reign of terror that lasted more than a year. When I protested the barbarism, I was deprived of all the rights of an American citizen and imprisoned in a military bastille for three months.

"West Virginia is on trial before the bar of the nation. The military arrests and the court-martial which I was forced to undergo in that state were the first move ever made by the ruling class to have the working class tried by the military and not civil courts. It is up to the American workers to make sure that it is the last. (*Now her voice takes on an edge*) What galled me most about my confinement at the military prison at Pratt, West Virginia, was the knowledge that a bunch of corporate lickspittles had the right to confine me! But I must be frank and tell you that the second thing that galled me was the silence of many here tonight who should have *shouted* out against the injustice! I would still be in prison if Senator Kern had not introduced his resolution calling for an investigation of conditions in West Virginia. No thanks, then, to *you* that I am here tonight! (*Now she is angry*) Cowards! Moral cowards! If you had only risen to your feet like men and said, 'We don't allow military despotism in America! Stop it!' A lot of moral cowards you are! Not a word of protest did we get out of you! Instead, you sat idly by and let these things be!" (*She rakes the audience with a fiery look. Then she drops the role and steps down from the platform, a bland look on her face*)

In January, 1921, a wonderful thing happened to me. I made a trip all the way down to Mexico City as the special guest of the Mexican government. The invitation was delivered by my old friend, Manuel Sarabia, who was now a high official in the Mexican government. The invitation said that the president of Mexico wanted to honor me for my help in the overthrow of the Porfirio Diaz dictatorship, and for my years of support for Mexican workers.

It was the first time in my life that I ever rode first class on the railroad. Not only that, I had my own Pullman car! It was provided by the Mexican government, and it was just for me—special conductor, special porters, special everything. I tell you it was really something!

It was a marvelous trip. I'd never traveled in Mexico, so most of the way I looked out the window of my bedroom and enjoyed the countryside as it went by. Every hour or so, the conductor would come to my door and ask if I was comfortable or if I needed anything or to tell me how soon we'd be in Mexico City. I tell you I felt like the Queen of Sheba.

On the last day of the trip, about forty miles from Mexico City, the train suddenly jolted to a stop. And we just sat there. After a few minutes I began to hear shouts from outside the train, and I got a little worried. I had heard that out in the open country of Mexico it wasn't unusual for bandits to stop the trains and rob the passengers.

I opened my window and leaned out to take a look. The first thing I saw was a string of taxi cabs and several buses blocking the tracks, right in front of the engine.

Then I saw a crowd of people—men, women, children— about two hundred of them, moving from railroad car to railroad car, as if they were looking for something or someone. Then they caught sight of me leaning out the window, and you wouldn't believe the roar that went up.

"*Madre Juanita!*" they shouted, pointing at me. "*Madre Juanita!*" And the whole crowd surged toward the car I was in. Just then the conductor stuck his head into my bedroom and explained what was going on. These people were strikers from a nearby factory and had commandeered just about every taxi cab and bus in the area so they could come and see me. By this time, they all were gathered outside my window, smiling up at me, many of them crying, some of them reaching up just to try to touch me. And I noticed that almost every one of them was carrying a bunch of flowers.

Then a lovely thing happened. Those closest to me began throwing their flowers through my open window. They fell back and the next line came up and threw more flowers through the window. They fell back and the next line came and so on. Within a few minutes my entire bedroom was *full* of flowers—roses, violets, carnations. And I was standing in flowers literally up to my waist. All the while the crowd kept chanting, "*Madre Juanita! (Her voice becomes softer) Madre Juanita! Madre Juanita!*" (*She pauses, smiling in reminiscence. Now, for the first time, there are hints of her age. Her posture is not quite so erect, she walks a bit more slowly and her voice is not quite so strong. There is a brief pause*) Today was my birthday. May One, 1930. I am 100 years old today. (*She pauses again. Then, almost in wonderment*) My God! 100 years old! (*She places both hands to her face, gently feeling the skin*) I know I *look* old, but I don't *feel* old. In my mind, I mean. Isn't that strange?

You know, it's peculiar what the brain does when you get to be my age. Sometimes I can't remember what happened five minutes ago. And yet I can remember so clearly I want to cry things that happened when I was a young girl. I remember the terrible fight I had with Papa and Mama about the young man I was seeing. Oh, how we hurt one another. I remember how I hated living in Canada, and I remember so well my first real teaching job in Michigan.

But you know what I resent? I finally resent age. I resent what age has done to me, finding myself unable to go where I should be going, do what I should be doing. When I read in the papers about a mine explosion or a steel mill strike, it's like a charge of electricity shoots through my head. My mind says—Let's go! Those boys need me! But . . . that's as far as it gets.

I live now with Walter and Lilly May Burgess here in Hyattsville, Maryland, near Washington. They're a lovely couple, the Burgesses. They take care of me like I was one of the family. It was Lilly May who planned the birthday party earlier today. I told her there was no need for all this fuss and bother, but she said of course there was, it was my 100th birthday; that when *she* got to be 100 she expected *me* to do the same for *her*. We both had a good laugh over that one.

Lilly May told me she'd invited a pretty sizeable bunch of people for the party, and that she expected people to be dropping in all day long. So I got up early this morning, dressed, had a little breakfast and by seven o'clock I was out in the front yard, sitting under the apple tree. It was a nice, warm spring morning and the birds were singing and I kept an eye on the road that led past the house. Pretty soon along came my first visitor. I didn't know who he was, but he was carrying a big bunch of flowers. He came into the yard, took off his hat, said good morning and said he was a retired coal miner from West Virginia who just wanted to wish me a happy birthday. Which he did. Then he handed me the flowers, shook my hand, put on his hat and left. That was the beginning. All day long they came. Three hundred twenty-five of 'em, Lilly May told me later. And she and Walter fed 'em all. There were tubs full of punch, dozens of cakes, cookies, sandwiches and I don't know what all. I don't mind saying I had a right good time.

The Movietone Newsreel people showed up with their camera and microphone. The director said that after he took a few shots of the distinguished guests, like the Vice President and Clarence Darrow, he would like to film me making a short speech of about forty-five seconds or so. I told him that I'd never made a forty-five-second speech in my life, but I'd give it a stab.

They took their other pictures and then were ready for me. The cameraman started the camera and the director motioned for me to begin. I looked right into the lens, as he had told me, and started. (*She moves close to the edge of the stage, stands just a bit straighter, her voice just a bit stronger. A spotlight hits her as all the other lights are doused. She stands in the bright spotlight for a moment, then:*)

"I want to send greetings to all my boys out there. You miners and steelworkers and all the rest of you. You know, boys, I have fought for you all my life, but now I'm facing my closing hours on this earth. My one regret is that I won't be around to help you younger fellahs the way I helped your fathers before some of you were born. You will face your own battles and another Mother Jones will take my place. And you are going to win! (*She pauses*) You hear what I say? You—are—going—to win!" (*She glares at the camera, the old fire in her eyes, as the spotlight slowly fades to black.*)

JOURNEYS
A Short Play

by Steve Schaeffer

The first runner-up in the second readers theatre competition is **Journeys,** a tragic prose-poem on domestic violence that packs an enormous emotional impact into remarkably few pages. Its author, Steve Schaeffer, of New York City, is a graduate of UCLA's School of Theatre, Film and Television and the University of Hull, England. "I began my career as a director," he said, "with my work appearing at Ensemble Studio Theatre, Playwrights Horizons Summerfest and the Lee Strasberg Institute in L.A., among other places." Other of his plays, including *The Followers, Bodies of Light* and a "comical musical tragedy," *Below the Valley of the Dolls*, have been performed both in this country and England.

The Open Book's New York production of **Journeys** opened at the Amsterdam Room on June 6, 1996, with the following cast:

WOMAN # 1	Kathryn Carrol
WOMAN # 2	Saralee Kaye
WOMAN # 3	Erin Maile Bortles

Characters

WOMAN 1: abused, aged 28
WOMAN 2: successful, aged 30
WOMAN 3: jailed, WOMAN 1 four years later

Scene

The play takes place in the living spaces and minds of the three women, representationally portrayed. There should not be any direct contact between the characters.

A Note on Violence

The violence of the play should be realistically portrayed, but only reactively from the side of the person speaking. At no time should one actor attack the other physically. During the lines that are all caps, the woman speaking is saying the lines of the husband. She should not also act out physically.

As the lights come up, Woman 1 is lying on the floor of her suburban home, Woman 2 is seated in hers, and Woman 3 is lying on a cot in her prison cell.

WOMAN 1: I wake up.

WOMAN 2: I wake up.

WOMAN 3: I wake up.

WOMAN 1: My eyes barely open. Swollen shut. Bright lights glaring. Sharp nails of light.

WOMAN 2: I've slept well. The day is bright and blue. I look forward to getting out today.

WOMAN 3: I feel the old panic try to grab me by the throat before I realize where I am and shake it off. The bright light seems gray. I can't sleep these days.

WOMAN 1: My head buzzes. I try to focus, to listen. I strain my ears to hear your sounds, your steps, your anger. Nothing. I close my eyes in relief. My heart loosens a little bit.

WOMAN 2: I look at you sleeping so soundly. I hate to disturb you. You look so innocent, like a little boy, all curled up and dreaming. So peaceful. I shake you awake.

WOMAN 3: I don't move for quite a while. I stay still. I stare at the black cracks in a gray ceiling. A web of fissures, small gaps to escape to. I let the cracks fill my mind.

WOMAN 1: I try to get up. Heat explodes into my brain, as I lift my head. My arm is a purple bruise. I think I'm going to

vomit. I hold my breath and stomach and close my eyes
tight, waiting for the feeling to go away.

WOMAN 2: We bump into each other as we prepare our break-
fasts. The kitchen is annoyingly small. The counters trap
us in like a prison cell. I hope we move into a bigger place
soon. It's about time. Of course, I don't have much time to
cook. I'm a very busy woman.

WOMAN 3: Now, in the early morning, I feel peace. Or something close to it. Just letting my mind remain empty, feeling no fear, no pain, just floating in a limbo of nothingness,
my eyes closed, shutting out the gray.

WOMAN 1: I stumble toward the bathroom, each step sending
bolts of hot steel through my aching muscles. I thought I'd
be used to the pain, but each time seems worse. I look in
the mirror. A hideous stranger stares back at me, face
purple, dried blood on her mouth. I begin to shake. That
can't be me! Oh, God, please don't let that be me!

WOMAN 2: I catch a glimpse of myself in my rearview mirror
on my way downtown. I'm a researcher for a medical firm.
It's very interesting work, although most people don't
think so. Whenever I tell anyone what I do, they look at
me like I'm from Mars. It's really amazing how little the
layperson really understands. I look good today. I feel
good.

WOMAN 3: An old woman looks at me from the mirror. Where
did she come from I wonder? She looks like my mother.
The prison bell rings, splitting my peace in two, allowing
all the ignored thoughts to enter my mind once again. I try
to shut them out, to keep the peace a little longer, but the
thoughts come racing in, chomping at the bit to get a piece

of my mind. I open my eyes, bringing me back to the gray nine-by-nine world I exist in. Yet still they come.

WOMAN 1: Tears I thought were gone come again, spilling down my cheeks, making my cuts sting. I try to shut them out. If only I could get through this minute, this hour, this day, this week, then I'd know what to do. I could make a plan to leave, to get out. But it's so hard to think. I hurt so much. And if you come back, if you're angry . . . it's so hard just to move. I don't know what to do.

WOMAN 2: Two evenings a week I spend at a women's center. I counsel all sorts of women and lead them to resources that can help them further. We get all kinds of cases. My friends have always said that I'm good with people, and I like to help.

WOMAN 3: Your voice is what I hear the most. It comes echoing to me, trying to bring me back. I fight against it. The voice I once loved so much. Now it reaches out for me relentlessly. I try to shut my mind against it, but it slips through, pulling me back.

WOMAN 1: Key turning in lock. Door opening. Heart racing. Stay still. I won't make you mad.

WOMAN 3: ARE YOU READY?

WOMAN 1: Your eyes so cold. Jaw tight. No look of love, no feeling that used to be there. A mask of rage, not the face I fell in love with. I can't see that face at all. I try to run away, to hide, to escape.

WOMAN 3: YOU WHORE! I'LL TEACH YOU A LESSON!

WOMAN 1: Head snaps against hard fist. Explosion of pain and confusion. What did I do? What did I—

WOMAN 3: DON'T TALK BACK TO ME, YOU SLUT!

WOMAN 1: Hands on throat, squeezing. Heart pounding, bursting. Head against wall. Bash, bash, bash, bash! Hot blood in my eyes. Everything going black. My head'll come right off! The world is a blur. I need to concentrate, to escape.

WOMAN 3: I'LL TEACH YOU!

WOMAN 1: Hard boot into soft flesh. A hole burns through my stomach. I need to breathe, to concentrate. If I can just breathe, it'll end. I can disappear, make it through. You'll have destroyed my body, but not my mind. I need to keep my mind. That's all I have left.

WOMAN 3: BITCH!

WOMAN 1: Pain . . .

WOMAN 3: SLUT!

WOMAN 1: Searing . . .

WOMAN 3: WHORE!

WOMAN 1: Something snaps. Sharp pain up my side. Something's broke. Harder to breathe. I think something's broke in me! I try to pull away, get away. I slide myself across the floor. Each move impossible. Hair pulled back, scalp stretched. Why are you doing this? I tried so hard to be good! A fire explodes in my mouth. I taste blood. Please stop! Oh, please!

WOMAN 3: I DON'T KNOW WHY I WASTE MY TIME WITH YOU. YOU'RE NOT WORTH IT!

WOMAN 1: Dropped to ground. Floor cold, hard. Need to move, can't. Think! You're gone, steps echo down hall. I need to disappear, to curl up inside myself. I try to breathe, to escape. You still don't have my mind!

WOMAN 3: YOU WANT TO BE A WHORE? THEN I'LL TREAT YOU LIKE ONE!

WOMAN 1: Black metal and wood in your hand. Gun! Oh, lord, you have a gun! You're going to kill me! You really are! I try to move away, too slow. No, please, no! On top of me, hot breath on my neck, weight holding me, crushing me. I try to move. Can't. Cold, black metal against my thighs, between my legs, pushing up. No! I try to squeeze, to shut it out. Tear of clothing. Hot breath. Blood pounding. Metal so cold. Weight crushing. Coldness in me, inside of me. Please, don't!

WOMAN 2: A woman came into the center today.

WOMAN 3: I tried to get help.

WOMAN 2: She was so scared, and looked like she'd been beaten although she tried to cover it with makeup.

WOMAN 3: I was so scared. What if you found me? What if you found out that I told? I tried not to shake.

WOMAN 2: She said her husband had hit her. That she didn't know what to do.

WOMAN 3: I knew I had to get out, but I didn't know how.

WOMAN 2: I asked her what she'd done, how the fight had started.

WOMAN 1: I don't know. He gets so mad. I didn't do anything.

WOMAN 2: Had it happened before?

WOMAN 1: Yes.

WOMAN 2: How many times?

WOMAN 1: I don't know. Too many to count.

WOMAN 3: She made me feel so stupid, so dirty.

WOMAN 2: I told her it was obvious she should leave him.

WOMAN 3: I had no money, no job. I couldn't get very far. I knew you'd find me. You always found me when I tried to leave before. There was so much I wanted to tell her, to make her understand—

WOMAN 1: He said he'd kill me if I tried to leave again! He has a gun. I know he'll do it.

WOMAN 3: But couldn't. The words wouldn't come.

WOMAN 2: She seemed to think it was impossible to leave him.

WOMAN 1: My family is the first place you'll look.

WOMAN 3: You knew where all my friends lived.

WOMAN 1: There's no place to go without you finding me.

WOMAN 3: And you'd be mad.

WOMAN 1: So, so mad.

WOMAN 2: She seemed to think he was all-powerful, almost omniscient. I gave her the address of a shelter in town that would have kept her for a month.

WOMAN 1: He'd find me.

WOMAN 3: Then what? She didn't understand.

WOMAN 2: I couldn't understand this woman. How could she live with this man? How could she let herself become so victimized by him? I'd never let you hit me. I would have packed my bags long ago.

WOMAN 3: You were so sorry at first. You'd cry when you saw how you had hurt me.

WOMAN 1: I'M SO SORRY. PLEASE BE ALL RIGHT. PLEASE BE ALL RIGHT AGAIN. I LOVE YOU SO MUCH. YOU KNOW THAT. OH, GOD, I'M SO SORRY.

WOMAN 3: And you'd hold me so close, and I was so hurt and confused. I wanted to believe you, to believe it would never happen again. I needed to be held so badly.

WOMAN 1: I'LL NEVER HURT YOU AGAIN. I PROMISE. I LOVE YOU.

WOMAN 2: I've always learned to be my own person. To never let anyone think they had power over me just because I was a woman and he was a man. What did this woman learn?

WOMAN 1: To be supportive and understanding.

WOMAN 3: To forgive and forget.

WOMAN 1: To put others' needs before your own.

WOMAN 3: To hold the family together.

WOMAN 1: To love.

WOMAN 3: Honor.

WOMAN 1: And obey.

WOMAN 2: I did all I could. I tried to understand. But what makes these women go back to these men? Don't they have any self-respect? I wish she would go to the shelter. She could get professional counseling there.

WOMAN 3: I could tell she thought there was something wrong with me. That it was my fault.

WOMAN 1: It's not my fault! I don't want this to happen to me. Do I?

WOMAN 3: I hated being beaten. But it had gone on for so long.

WOMAN 1: I can't remember how it feels to hope. To not feel pain.

WOMAN 3: I was so weak and hurt all the time.

WOMAN 1: I think you'll kill me soon. Just beat me until I die. Sometimes I welcome the thought.

WOMAN 3: I thought the next time I might die.

WOMAN 1: FUCKING BITCH!

WOMAN 3: You'd been drinking. You were angrier than I'd ever seen you. Fear raced through me. Your eyes were blue steel; your face, a mask of unfeeling hate. You came after me. I tried to run. I was so hurt already, I didn't think I could take much more.

WOMAN 1: I CAN'T TRUST YOU! I JUST CAN'T TRUST YOU!

WOMAN 2: I made it as far as the living room. You grabbed my arm and threw me across the room. I crashed into the end table, breaking the leg off—almost breaking *my* leg off. I tried to scramble to my feet, but my head was spinning. You grabbed me. Your fist crashed against my skull again and again and again. I could feel the hot blood running down my face and into my ears. You wouldn't stop. You were going to kill me! You really were!

WOMAN 1: WHY DID I MARRY SUCH AN UGLY SLUT? WHY?

WOMAN 3: You picked me up and threw me against the wall. My back slammed straight against it, leaving a spray of cracks where I hit. My teeth clamped hard on my tongue; I could taste my own blood. I couldn't take much more. My body was a capsule of pain. Then I saw it.

WOMAN 1: I'M GOING TO KILL YOU, YOU BITCH! I'M GOING TO KILL YOU WITH MY OWN HANDS!

WOMAN 3: The gun. Lying in back of the couch, forgotten. I staggered towards it, almost falling, almost blacking out. I picked it up, struggling for consciousness. It felt heavy and cold in my hands. I pointed it at you. I begged you to stop. Please, stop!

WOMAN 1: GO AHEAD! GO AHEAD AND SHOOT ME!

WOMAN 3: You took a step forward. The gun went off. And I blacked out. When I came to a few minutes later, I kept thinking, "He's going to be so mad now! He's going to be so mad!" But you didn't come after me. You were sprawled across the floor. And there was so much blood. I didn't know what to do. I had to get help. I couldn't have killed you. You couldn't really be dead! But you were.

WOMAN 2: I was watching the news. I saw a story about a woman who had murdered her husband. She shot him five times. My blood ran cold when I saw her. It was a woman who came into the center once. I had talked to her.

WOMAN 3: I don't even remember doing it. The gun just went off. I don't know how many times.

WOMAN 2: I remember how scared she was. She was so scared, but she wouldn't leave her husband. She said he had hit her.

WOMAN 3: It all happened so fast. I didn't know what I was doing. It just went off.

WOMAN 2: I couldn't believe it.

WOMAN 3: I don't remember it happening.

WOMAN 2: She didn't look like a murderer.

WOMAN 3: I don't remember it at all. Except . . .

WOMAN 2: That night . . .

WOMAN 3: Late at night . . .

WOMAN 2: I had a dream . . .

WOMAN 3: Almost like a dream . . .

WOMAN 2: We were in the kitchen. Trapped together by the counters.

WOMAN 3: I'm back in our house. You've just thrown me against the wall. I can taste my blood and I see the gun. I run to it. I pick it up.

WOMAN 2: You turned towards me. Your eyes were blue steel; your face a mask of unfeeling hate.

WOMAN 3: The gun feels heavy and cold in my hand. And powerful. I feel so powerful. Part of me is scared and yells for you to stop, but the rest of me feels the strength of the gun. I want you to step forward. I want you to.

WOMAN 2: I see the blur of your fist as it comes down against my face.

WOMAN 3: I feel the trigger against my finger. I see you step toward me. And in that moment, I hate you. There's not hurt or fear or pain anymore, just blind hate for everything you did to me. For every kick and hit and bruise and scream. I pull the trigger. I know exactly what I'm doing.

WOMAN 2: My head snapped back, a burst of pain and confusion. I was thrown sideways, bruising my hip against the counter. You stepped towards me. I was trapped; no escape. What did I do? Please tell me what I did!

WOMAN 3: I feel so strong as I see you reel from the bullet. Your face changes. Instead of hate, there is surprise and confusion. And that look turns to fear when I pull the trigger again. *You're* afraid of *me* now. You're helpless. I can do anything to you I want. My heart almost breaks from the overwhelming feeling I feel as I pull the trigger again and again. I watch as your life bleeds from you, and I feel something I hadn't felt in years: joy.

WOMAN 2: I wake up.

WOMAN 3: I try to sleep, to forget.

WOMAN 2: I'm trembling. I feel so cold as I look at you curled up beside me.

WOMAN 3: I feel so empty inside. Like all my feelings have been drained away. If only I could forget.

WOMAN 2: Of course it was only a dream. I try to forget.

WOMAN 3: I don't want to remember those feelings. I want to forget I ever had them, forget they were ever a part of me, but I can't. It's almost worse than the pain, the beatings. Because I always thought—

WOMAN 1: I can't let you get my mind. You'll have had my body, but not my mind. That's mine. It's all I have left.

WOMAN 3: But those feelings. The blind fury and hate. The joy in being able to hurt you back. I felt them. I tasted them. But they're yours, not mine. I never wanted them. I want to give them back, but can't.

WOMAN 2: I haven't forgotten that dream.

WOMAN 3: Because during those moments when I held your life in my hands—

WOMAN 2: I can't look at you the same now. It's as if I saw something I never knew was there, and I keep fearing it will return.

WOMAN 3: Each time I pulled the trigger, you turned me into what you were. You turned me into a monster whose only pleasure was to inflict pain. And somehow I think you knew. You stole away a part of me. Or made me find something inside myself that I didn't want to know about. And I can't forgive you for that. I can't forgive myself.

WOMAN 1: I feel so hurt all the time.

WOMAN 3: I close my eyes tight against the memory.

WOMAN 2: I close my eyes and try to forget.

WOMAN 1: I close my eyes and slip into darkness.

ALL: But you're still there.

WOMAN 3: You've thrown me against the wall, leaving a spray of cracks in the plaster.

WOMAN 2: I see the cold mask of your face. I feel the burst of pain and confusion in my head.

WOMAN 1: You face is like a mask, glowing in my dreams. I can't escape you even then.

WOMAN 3: The mask of hate covers your features, as overwhelming rage takes you over the edge of humankindness.

WOMAN 2: The sink holes that were once your eyes pierce their way into me and deaden my soul.

WOMAN 1: I go to a lonely island of pain where the voices of despair cry—

WOMAN 2: This can't be happening again!

WOMAN 1: Where the waters of forgetfulness lap the shores of my consciousness.

WOMAN 2: There are cracks in the plaster of my life. I thought I knew you.

WOMAN 3: I shake my eyes open and stare at black cracks in a gray ceiling.

WOMAN 1: Until I remember the trick of jumping out of my body so that I can slip through the crack in the wall where my soul becomes whole again.

WOMAN 3: I wait.

WOMAN 1: The fury will subside.

WOMAN 3: I ride the current.

WOMAN 2: The mask will dissolve and melt back into your face.

WOMAN 1: I return to untie the knots in my stomach, to ice the burning of my bruises. To face the aftermask.

WOMAN 3: The calm after the storm . . .

WOMAN 2: A relief . . .

WOMAN 1: But my eyes scan the wall, mapping the spot where the crack appeared. For I know in the dark corner of my heart that I will have to make the journey yet another time.

(Lights fade to black. End of play.)

THE END OF A LINE

A One-act Play

by Robert Hawkins

Third place winner Robert Hawkins moves up one slot from the place taken by his full-length domestic comedy-drama, *Quiet! Three Ladies Laughing*, in the first national readers theatre competition. A native of Alabama, Mr. Hawkins began as a cub reporter for the same City News Bureau of Chicago that produced Ben Hecht and Charles MacArthur's *The Front Page*. Later, says Hawkins, "I worked for the *Chicago Tribune*, but during midlife crisis, became a reporter for the *Northern Territory News* in Darwin, Australia, before settling into a twenty-plus-year career as an IBM writer/editor." Now retired, the playwright lives in St. Augustine, Florida, where he is an assistant professor of communications at Flagler College.

The Open Book's New York readers theatre production of **The End of a Line** opened June 6, 1996, at the Amsterdam Room with the following cast:

MARGARET GRAVLEE, *the older sister*	Jennifer Daniels
NORA (GRAVLEE) ASHTON, *the younger sister*	Nancy Temple
MASON MILLER, *the visitor*	Eric Bryant

Cast

(In order of appearance)

Margaret Gravlee	The older sister
Nora (Gravlee) Ashton	The younger sister
Mason Miller	The visitor

The modest living room in a home shared by two elderly sisters, Nora Ashton and Margaret Gravlee in Birmingham, Alabama. The room is crammed with antiques. A large round table is near the center of the room. Two rotating fans whir on the floor.

AT RISE: *Nora, alone in room, nervously knits. After a few moments, Margaret enters and starts straightening things in the room. She, too, is nervous.*

MARGARET: Now remember, Nora. Don't ask this young man a lot of personal questions . . . or tell him anything about us. Just let me do the talking.

NORA: You always do!

MARGARET: Nora . . . we both know that you have a way of telling complete strangers things about the family they have no business knowing whatsoever.

NORA: I do not! . . . It's just that I sometimes have a hard time making small talk and I may . . . say things . . . that I probably shouldn't, but I don't . . . (*Nora goes back to knitting, but abruptly drops it in her lap*) Oh, Margaret . . . I don't think I can go through with this . . . is he going to . . . is he going to just *bring* him right in!

MARGARET: Nora, please! Control yourself.

NORA: I'll try . . .

(*A knock at the door*)

NORA: Oh! (*Nora drops her knitting and looks flustered. Margaret rushes to pick up her sewing basket, gives Nora the once over to see if she is neat. Another knock at the door. Nora dashes offstage*)

MARGARET: Nora! Come back here! (*Margaret goes to door, braces herself and adjusts her brooch. She wipes her forehead, wet with perspiration, and walks bravely to the front door . . . hesitates a moment and then opens it firmly*)

MARGARET: Yes?

MILLER: Good afternoon. I'm Mason Miller.

MARGARET: Good afternoon Mr. Miller. My sister and I have been expecting you. Please, come in. I'm Margaret Gravlee.

(*Margaret makes a gesture with her hand and holds the door open. Miller enters with a carry-on sized bag. He steps inside, dripping wet with perspiration. His suit is rumpled, tie askew. He's disappointed to find it not much cooler inside*)

MILLER: Whew! It's so humid! It gets hot in New York, but . . . wow! Not like this. Now I know what they're talking about when they talk about an Alabama summer!

MARGARET: It is rather warm today . . . and it has been all summer. May I take your coat? (*Takes it and hangs it up*) I hope you won't be too uncomfortable . . . our air conditioner chose this moment not to work. Wouldn't you just know? Please . . . do have a seat.

MILLER: Thank you . . .

MARGARET: I don't know where my sister Nora has gotten to.

MILLER: I hope that my delaying this trip last week hasn't put you to any trouble. Some personal matters came up at the last minute I had to attend to.

MARGARET: No trouble at all. It's very considerate of you to come in the first place. This has been quite upsetting to me . . . and my sister. We really didn't know what to expect . . . oh, excuse me. You must think I have no manners at all. May I offer you some iced tea? Have you had luncheon?

MILLER: Oh . . . iced tea would be fine. I don't have any appetite in this heat.

MARGARET: Make yourself at home. I'll make a few sandwiches in case you change your mind . . . I'll only be a moment.

MILLER: Take your time . . . (*Margaret leaves and Miller looks around the room. He spots a photograph of a relative on the side table, looks at it and then remembers his bag. As he opens it and pulls out a cardboard box, Nora enters and sees him with the box. When he spots her, he shoves the box back into the bag*) Why . . . hello. You must be Mrs. Ashton.

(*Nora hesitates, then smiles*)

NORA: I am . . . and you must be Mr. . . . Mr. Miller.

MILLER: Yes.

(*An awkward pause. Nora's attention returns to the bag he has brought. Miller clears his throat and continues*)

MILLER: Your sister's getting some tea. . . . These portraits here . . . I was wondering . . . who is this fine-looking gentleman? He sure looks a lot like Bill.

NORA (*coming out of her daze*): Oh . . . that's my great-great-grandfather . . . Williamson Gravlee . . . one of the first settlers of this valley. It wasn't called Birmingham then, you know. That came much later.

MILLER: I take it Bill was named for him?

NORA: Bill?

MILLER: Yes . . . uhh . . . Bill, your nephew. (*Miller laughs*) I mean, Williamson. I forgot. We never called Bill by that name. Williamson Welton Gravlee III! That's a bit too grand . . . even for us jaded New Yorkers.

NORA: That's strange. We would have never called young Williamson . . . Bill. Oh, please sit down, Mr. Miller.

MILLER: Please . . . call me Mason.

NORA: I rather like it . . .

MILLER: What?

NORA: Bill . . . I know Williamson Sr. hated his name. He called himself Wim . . . said it was better for business to shorten it. My sister Margaret thought it was in such poor taste to ruin such a beautiful and prestigious name.

MILLER: Wim . . . I like that. But, I suppose it's all what you get used to. To me, Bill was Bill. Not a William, mind you. And he certainly wasn't a Williamson. At least in New York. But, he could have been a Wim . . . yeah!

NORA: Oh, he was such a delightful child! (*Picks up another photo*) Just like my brother . . . and handsome! Like father, like son. They both were handsome men.

(Nora slips into a reverie with a pained look on her face. Miller tries to change the subject)

MILLER: It sure is warm today. I'm sorry your air conditioning is on the blink.

NORA: Oh . . . we don't have air conditioning.

MILLER: You don't?

NORA: No . . . I tried to talk Margaret into at least getting a unit for each of our bedrooms, but she wouldn't hear of it. Said it was too much money . . . too much money. . . . It's my money anyway . . .

MILLER: I didn't mean to be rude, I just thought your air conditioning wasn't working.

NORA: Didn't think that memorial for Elizabeth . . . our great-great-grandmother . . . was too much money . . . and she was a Yankee! *(Nora laughs)* La-a-a . . . she came all the way down here from Connecticut in 1826 to teach school. *(Nora hurries over to the portrait wall)* This is her . . . right here. Her sister Charlotte came later . . . that's Charlotte over there. . . . They both married local men, one being my great-grandfather, of course. Elizabeth kept a diary about her journey down here on a sailing ship from New York to Mobile, then up the Warrior River by flat boat . . . oh, it's quite a story, a real adventure for such a cultured young lady from Waterbury. Have you ever been to Waterbury?

MILLER: Uhh . . . yes . . . but I . . . I've never stopped off . . . uhh . . .

NORA: I've always wanted to see it . . . just the name sounds so lovely! Water-bury! I probably won't get the chance to go now and, of course, we don't have any relatives there any more to stay with. They're all dead and gone . . . you know how Southerners are. We never stay in a hotel as long as there's a relative within shouting distance.

MILLER (*clearing his throat*): Oh, uhh . . . I have reservations at the Tutwiler Hotel for tonight.

NORA: Oh! . . . We were expecting you to stay with us tonight. Aren't you? Didn't Margaret mention it to you? We have Williamson's . . . oh why don't I say, Bill . . . we have Bill's room already made up for you.

MILLER: She may have mentioned it, but my secretary has made reservations . . .

NORA: Ah shaw . . . it would be no trouble at all. We never have guests any more. Oh, I miss not having a lot of people around. This ole house doesn't have much room . . . not like my big house over in Montevallo. I miss that house. Sometimes I'm sorry I let Margaret talk me into selling it and buying this place. If the truth were known, I really don't like it here. None of the furniture fits . . . it's so cramped.

MILLER: How long have you and Miss Gravlee lived together?

NORA: About 10 years. You see, Margaret never married. She had a small apartment for years after we lost the old homestead. It made sense for us to live together. Oh, Margaret could have married, but . . . (*whispering carefully*) My late husband said she never thought any of her beaus had the proper background. . . . (*Resumes normal speech*) Mr. Ashton, my husband, died thirty years ago in Septem-

ber. The 28th, to be exact. Just keeled over and died. It's
better that way, I think. I always called him Mr. Ashton
because I never liked his first name. It was Burr. I found it
hard to say.

MILLER: Burr? Like in Aaron Burr?

NORA: Oh, mercy, yes! His great-grandfather was the first
Burr Ashton. Oh, it's a mar-r-velous story. Move that fan
around so that it blows on you . . . it is so hot today. Oh,
in spite of what Margaret says, I think I'm just gonna call
up Sears and have 'em send me out an air conditioner.
(*They sit*) Now, where was I? Oh . . . I was telling you
something . . . I'm getting so addled . . .

MILLER: Aaron Burr . . . you were going to tell me about
how your husband got that name.

NORA: Oh, yes . . . Mr. Burr, of course, was once the vice
president of the United States. I forget the year. But, he
had committed some horrible crime . . . I think it was
treason. Anyway, he was fleeing from somewhere, Washington, I guess . . . everybody flees Washington sooner
or later, I always say . . . He was trying to get to Texas
. . . or was it Mexico? Anyway, some far away place. But
just after he crossed over into Mississippi, he was captured
by federal troops. Well, they were dragging him back for a
trial and this terrible storm came up. Oh, it was awful! So
they stopped at our house, or rather the Ashton homestead
over there in Shelby County. And wouldn't you know it!
My husband's great-grandmother was just giving birth
. . . and it was a boy! So, they named him in honor of the
vice president! They didn't know Mr. Burr was a criminal
and on the run from the law!

(Nora laughs heartily. Margaret enters, frowns at the laughter, but regains her composure)

MARGARET: Nora . . . there you are . . . would you please clear the table?

(Nora stops laughing. She's embarrassed about being called down)

NORA: Would you excuse me, Mr. Miller . . .

(Nora removes a bowl of flowers from the table while glaring at Margaret as she puts down the tea tray. Nora exits in a huff)

MARGARET *(motioning for him to sit down at the table)*: Please excuse Nora . . . she's very upset today.

MILLER: Oh, I understand. But I find her so charming . . . and she tells a great story, too.

MARGARET: Yes . . . *(under her breath)* I know. *(Resumes)* We always go ahead and sweeten the tea. Would you care for lemon?

MILLER: Yes, please.

(Margaret hands Miller a plate of lemons. They are both uncomfortable and wait for the other to speak)

MARGARET: How long did you know Williamson, Mr. Miller?

MILLER: Please . . . call me Mason. Oh . . . for a number of years, but I only really got to know him well after Marvin died. Marvin I knew from college . . . we came to New York together. Did you . . . ever meet Marvin?

MARGARET: No . . . but I knew of him.

MILLER: Funny? I was sure the two of you had met. He and
Bill were together for such a long time. You know, the
more I think of it, they were really the perfect couple.

MARGARET (*squirming in her chair*): Mr. Miller . . . if you
don't mind . . .

MILLER: I'm sorry. Did . . . did I say something wrong? I
didn't mean to offend you. You did know they . . . I . . .

MARGARET: I knew as much as I wanted to . . . I really don't
care to know . . . *everything!*

MILLER: I guess I've lived in New York too long. I forget
there's a whole different world outside of Manhattan . . .

MARGARET: I knew about this Marvin . . . I can't seem to
recall his last name . . .

MILLER: Katz . . . Marvin Katz.

MARGARET: Yes . . . that was it. A few years ago Williamson
. . . and this Marvin Katz . . . came by on their way to
the Mardi Gras. Williamson wanted me to meet him, but I
. . . I wasn't well. So, I didn't ask him to come in.

MILLER: That's a pity . . . Everyone liked Marvin. He was
such a talented guy. I loved him from the moment I met
him.

MARGARET (*harshly*): Would you care for more tea?

MILLER: No . . . no thank you . . .

112   FROM PAGE TO STAGE

(Both realize a stand off. Margaret stands up and begins to pace the room. Miller begins to feel ill at ease)

MARGARET: I don't mean to be rude . . . or prudish . . . but you have to realize I am from an entirely different world. . . . I find it so difficult to accept so many things that you . . . people like you . . . accept so readily.

MILLER: Like the idea that two people of the same sex can love one another?

MARGARET (*adamant*): People of the same sex "can" love one another . . . like father and son . . . or mother and daughter . . . brother and brother. But not . . . oh, you'll have to excuse me, Mr. Miller. I'm still having a hard time handling this . . . this . . .

(Nora enters the room, unsteadily)

MILLER: You were aware that he had been ill for some time, weren't you?

MARGARET: Well, I wasn't sure of the nature of his illness.

NORA: Margaret . . . that's not true and you know it! He wrote you about it last winter and you didn't answer him. (*To Marvin*) She threw the letter away without even letting me read it!

MARGARET: Nora . . . please! Remember what I said.

NORA: Margaret put it right there in the *Birmingham News* that he died from cancer.

MARGARET: Down here, Mr. Miller, we try not to air our dirty linen in public. There are some things that should be kept . . . private.

NORA: She means it's o.k. to die from cancer . . . or a heart attack . . . (*sadly*) oh . . . so many in our family in the early years died from TB . . . but most of them just lost their minds . . .

MARGARET (*warning tone*): Nor . . . a!

NORA: Well . . . they did. But young Williamson . . . I mean, Bill . . . Oh, why do I find it hard to remember that . . . Bill's father—our brother—threw himself out of a hotel window . . .

MARGARET: NORA!!!

NORA: I mean . . . he fell from a hotel window . . . it was an accident, you know. The police said so . . . but when Williamson told me later that he and his father had quarreled earlier, well . . . I wondered if . . .

MARGARET: Please!

NORA: I know . . . I talk too much. Please excuse me, Mr. Miller.

MILLER: Please call me Mason.

NORA: Yes, I'll remember that . . . Mason. Excuse me.

(*Nora exits. Margaret stares at her with a smoldering look*)

MARGARET: I hate to make excuses for Nora, but she does tend to run on at times . . .

MILLER: I think she's more delightful than Bill said. He used to tell me some marvelous stories about her.

MARGARET: About Nora? What on earth did he say?

MILLER: Oh, it was towards the end there when I was . . .
spending so much time with him. His mind wandered a
lot, but he often talked about his Aunt Nora's farm . . .
and how he was such a regular Tom Sawyer . . . swim-
ming in the creek, riding an ole mule . . . doing all those
things boys do. He seemed very close to your sister . . .
very close.

MARGARET: Well, his mother, Celia, was never really well . . .
and after she died . . . his father was on the road all the
time . . . well, he enjoyed the farm so much . . . it
really seemed best he stayed there . . . with Nora. (*Ut-
ters a little laugh*) Funny . . . I was just thinking about
the time he stayed with me when Nora's husband died. He
wanted to be at Nora's then, but he'd been exposed to too
many deaths . . . I wanted him with me for a while. One
day I took him out to the old fairgrounds where they had a
Merry-Go-Round. Oh! He was crazy about that ride . . .
I couldn't get him off, so I let him ride and ride . . . all
afternoon. That night when we came home, he sat down at
the piano and played that carousel tune by heart! Oh, he
had talent all right. I saw that! . . . Long ago . . .
(*smiles to herself*) I would have loved to have kept him
with me . . . to teach him . . . but I had a small apartment . . . I couldn't do it. (*A moment of tenderness*)
Thank you . . . we never did thank you for taking care of
him at the end.

MILLER: Well, I had a good teacher. I saw how Bill took care
of Marvin. He really had his hands full on that score . . .
playing at the club all night . . . taking care of Marvin
during the day . . . I don't see how he did it all.

MARGARET (*stiffening up at the mention of Marvin's name*): I
know very little about Williamson's life in New York and I

really don't want to. Walking away from that full scholarship at Juilliard . . . Oh, just to *throw it away!* I'll never forgive him for that!

MILLER: He didn't throw away his talent . . . he had style. He could play a Cole Porter tune better than . . . better than Bobby Short.

MARGARET: Cole Porter tunes! O-o-h! Mr. Miller, I'm not talking about some player of popular songs. Williamson could have become a major concert pianist . . . he could have played anywhere in the world! He just threw away his one big chance and that's usually all we get in this life . . . one big chance!

MILLER: Maybe he realized that being a concert pianist wasn't what he really wanted out of life.

MARGARET: You're wrong, Mr. Miller. If he hadn't met . . . that . . . that person! Oh, he was a bad influence on Williamson! He turned his life upside down!

MILLER: *That's not true!* If anything, Marvin was a good influence. Bill was going through some pretty tough emotional times when he met Marvin, so you've at least gotta give Marvin credit for helping him snap out of it and enjoy life a bit more . . .

MARGARET: Enjoy life more? This is what I mean, Mr. Miller. You people seem to think life is just for personal enjoyment. Well! Where do you fit things like honor, duty and responsibility to one's family into your scheme of things?

MILLER: How about duty and responsibility to one's self? Doesn't that count for anything?

MARGARET: That's what's wrong with the world today. All this me . . . me . . . me philosophy! (*Nora enters the room, wobbling again, obviously from having taken a drink or two*) Williamson uttered your very words when he dropped out of the University to "find himself" as he called it . . . in San Francisco of all places!

MILLER: San Francisco?

NORA: Oh, yes . . . what year was that? Oh, I forget . . . but it was a terrible time for all of us. Even his father was disgusted with him. He went out there to bring him home . . . and then that terrible incident at the hotel happened . . .

(*Dead silence*)

MARGARET: Nora . . . I think Mr. Miller has heard enough about that.

MILLER: Hmmm . . . maybe that explains why Bill would never honor any request at the bar for a song about San Francisco . . . Hmmm . . . I thought Bill came straight from Birmingham to Juilliard. I had no idea he lived in San Francisco . . .

NORA: Oh, no . . . he came back to the farm and rested up before going to Juilliard. He was so worn out . . . tired . . . so mixed up. It was almost a year before he took up the piano again . . . after Margaret forced . . . (*Nora stops short before making another faux pas*)

MARGARET: It was what saved him . . . for the time being. He had the talent . . . but not the discipline. (*Aimed at Nora*) Yes . . . you can even say I pushed him, but it was for his own good!

MILLER: I keep forgetting that you taught piano.

NORA: Oh, Margaret studied piano in New York, too.

MILLER: At Juilliard?

MARGARET: No, I took private lessons, but things were different in my time. Women had little chance of success in a
profession dominated by men. Perhaps now . . . but not
in my day. But I'm sure Williamson could have made it if
he had followed through. He could have made a name for
himself . . . he could have made us proud.

MILLER: Is that what he really wanted?

MARGARET: Of course that's what he wanted! We are a family
of achievers, Mr. Miller. French Huguenots from Charleston . . . settlers who brought culture and refinement to a
backwoods community. Oh yes . . . we come from a long
line of prominent physicians, judges . . . ministers, people of great accomplishments. And Williamson could have
followed in that tradition, too. He was the last male in the
Gravlee line . . . there are *no more males!*

MILLER: What did Bill's father do?

MARGARET (*hesitating*): He . . . he was a representative of
one of the south's largest manufacturers . . .

NORA: He sold chicken feed. (*Margaret sighs audibly*) Well, he
did . . . but it didn't work out. He . . . had a number of
traveling sales jobs . . . but he never seemed to be interested in them. Oh, he just never was right after he came
back from serving overseas during the war. (*Sadly*) He
drank so much then . . . couldn't stop, really.

MARGARET: Nora . . . you're trying my patience . . .

NORA: I know . . . but I'm telling the truth which is something you don't like to hear, Margaret. Wim drank. He drank a lot. I think that's what killed Celia, Williamson's mother. Oh, she tried to keep up with him, but she couldn't, God rest her soul.

MARGARET: I'm not going to put up with this. You're completely out of control and you know why.

NORA: I know . . . I know. It runs in the family. You see, Mr. . . . I mean, Mason . . . see, I did remember your name. Yes, I've had a few sips of sherry. I needed it . . . (*Nora dashes out again. Margaret does a slow burn. Miller stands up*)

MILLER: Perhaps I should leave. I didn't mean to . . .

MARGARET: Please . . . Mr. Miller. You haven't finished your tea. Nora's gotten very high strung lately . . . and she's depending on alcohol a little too much lately. That's why I wanted her to move here so I can keep an eye on her. Alcohol . . . uhhh! It's been a curse upon our whole family.

MILLER: Well, at least Bill didn't drink.

MARGARET: Didn't drink? Mr. Miller, he was a complete wreck when he returned from San Francisco. And I've always suspected that alcohol wasn't the only problem.

MILLER: That's funny. I never saw Bill have so much as a glass of wine unless it was a special occasion. And Marvin never drank. Perhaps Marvin was a good influence.

MARGARET: Well . . . he certainly influenced him in other ways . . . (*Nora enters with two glasses*) After that dreadful San Francisco venture, he was getting on the right track again towards his career . . . and I feel sure he was about to start a family.

MILLER (*utter disbelief*): A family?

MARGARET: Well, I know he met someone in San Francisco and was thinking . . . of getting married. And then . . .

NORA: Margaret, that's a boldface lie! (*Motions to Miller*) May I pour you a taste of this excellent sherry? I've been saving it for a very special occasion. This seems to be it.

(*Miller looks at Margaret, then answers*)

MILLER: No . . . no thank you.

NORA: Getting married indeed! Williamson told me . . . confidentially . . . that he . . . oh, well, I guess its all right to say it now . . . that he was . . . (*whispering to Miller, almost inaudible to the audience*) He was . . . (homo-)

MARGARET (*shocked beyond words*): U-h-h-h-h!

(*Margaret exits hurriedly in disgust. Nora lets out a sigh of despair*)

NORA: There I go . . . why do I always say the wrong things?

MILLER: Sometimes the truth hurts.

NORA: It sure seems to hurt Margaret . . . you know, she could never face up to how things really were . . . she always looked at how she thought things ought to be. But, it just doesn't work that way, does it.

MILLER: Not for me . . . or a lot of people I know.

NORA: Maybe Margaret should have been a man.

MILLER: A man?

NORA: I think she'd have been happier . . . I mean she could control things better. Control people better, too. Like . . . after a while, nobody listens to what she says. She can only intimidate you . . . and make you feel sorry about not doing things her way, but that's about all. I've come to understand that. But, if she were a man, she could really force you to do her bidding. (*Nora pauses*) My husband always could. I never told anyone this, but I was always afraid of Mr. Ashton.

MILLER: Afraid?

NORA: Yes . . . and I learned not to question a thing he said . . . not like women do today. (*Reflects*) I don't think I really loved him either. Oh, I respected him, but no, I didn't really love him. I don't think I would have even married him if it weren't for Margaret.

MILLER: What did she have to do with it?

NORA: Well . . . it was his family background that she harped on. Actually, he was a distant cousin . . . but they had money . . . not a lot, but comfortable, so Margaret thought we were the perfect match. She arranged the whole thing and I probably should have spoken up, but I thought she knew best. I tell you, where money is involved, Margaret takes charge.

MILLER: You didn't have any children, did you?

NORA: No . . . we didn't. That's why I was so close to . . . Bill. He was like my own child. (*Nora starts to cry as Margaret enters. Nora jumps up and rushes towards her as if to stop her before she speaks*) I must speak! I just can't keep denying it . . . Williamson died from AIDS! (*Dead silence*) There . . . I said it . . . out loud . . . *and in this house!* (*Margaret turns away and Nora gains composure*) It's nothing to be ashamed of . . . a lot of famous people have died from it, Margaret. Prominent people! After Bill wrote me about his illness I made a special trip down to the library and asked Miss Cauthen to get me all the information available on the subject.

MARGARET (*aghast*): You did what? Oh no! You asked that gossipy ole Miss Cauthen to do that? God only knows what she thought.

NORA: Well . . . I know she didn't think I had it!

MARGARET: That's not what I mean. She could put two and two together and well . . . it's too late now to care what she thought.

NORA: I wanted to know what it was all about. Bill was our nephew. I wanted to know the truth . . . and I don't care what anyone thinks . . . especially Miss Cauthen. And, I wanted *us* to be there at the end, too!

MILLER: He wanted you to be there . . . both of you but he didn't want you to be upset. You might not have recognized him . . . he lost so much weight . . .

(Nora straightens up some, and takes a handkerchief from her pocket and blows her nose)

NORA: Oh . . . it wouldn't have mattered. I just wanted to see him. He used to call a lot, but near the end he couldn't even hold up the phone. Tell me . . . what was it like . . . there at the end?

MILLER: Well, he was at home, you know. Both he and Marvin were lucky enough to die at home. You never did see the co-op they owned, did you? It was gorgeous with a view of the Hudson, a rooftop garden where Bill grew all those southern dall-yah's as he called them. It was a lucky thing that Marvin inherited tons of money!

(Margaret reacts as though she was struck by a bolt of lightning)

MARGARET: Money? What *money???*

MILLER: From Marvin's grandfather . . . Marvin was quite well off . . . I think it would be safe to say he was a millionaire, but you'd never know it. He never talked about money. I just know I was quite surprised at the little gift he left me. Everything else went to Bill.

MARGARET: *Went to Williamson? How . . . how much money?*

MILLER: I don't know the exact amount, but with both Marvin and Bill being at home during their long illnesses, I'm sure it took a lot of it. But, I do know that Bill left the remainder to a hospice.

(Margaret lets out a muffled cry of anguish. She is devastated and begins walking up and down, plotting)

NORA: Oh, that was so thoughtful . . . and, I'm so glad that he died peacefully at home. I just wish we'd have a little service here. . . . Can't we Margaret?

MILLER: We had one in New York . . . I thought you knew. I wanted both of you there . . .

NORA: Why Margaret, you didn't even mention that. (*Nora looks accusingly at Margaret*)

MARGARET: Nora . . . you know we couldn't have gone to that expense. We simply don't have the money! Besides, I thought it was best to have a religious service there . . . with his friends . . . and then . . . well, we can have a small graveside service up at St. Andrews. . . . When Mr. Miller told me that he would attend to the cremation . . . and even bring the remains here himself, well . . . I thought it was most generous. You remember how that funeral director out in San Francisco overcharged us in shipping Williamson Sr.'s body back here. I'll never get over that.

MILLER (*trying to smooth things*): I want you to know we had a beautiful service at the church in the Village where Bill used to attend regularly. Especially when Marvin got sick. It was packed to the rafters with both their friends . . . and all the guys who knew Bill down at the bar. But what really made it special was that just about every musician in the Village showed up, too . . . and a lot of them played Bill's favorites. . . . It was even written up in the *Village Voice*. Here, I brought several copies . . . (*Miller rummages through the flight bag and hands it to Nora. Nora starts skimming the article and puts it down, holding back tears*)

NORA: Oh . . . this is so nice. Usually obituaries are so sad
. . . so final. I don't like them. They never seem to cap-
ture the whole person . . . or talk about those little
things that made a person so special. They're like status
reports . . . this person was born here . . . lived there
. . . died somewhere else. Usually very short.

MARGARET (*with emphasis*): Unless they had truly accomplished something during their lifetime. Then there never
seems to be enough space to fit it all in.

NORA: Oh, Margaret . . . let it be. Please. Let's just remember Williamson as he was to each of us . . .

MARGARET: You think I'm so cruel and hardhearted. Well, I'm
not. I loved him, too! But he was our last hope . . . our
very last hope to make the Gravlee name stand for something!

NORA: Margaret, nobody cares about all that anymore! It's not
important! There's no black mark against our name for
something any of us have done. You certainly haven't done
anything and I did the best I could with my life . . . even
if it was only to marry Mr. Ashton. I think I made him
happy. I was reasonably happy . . . that's about all one
can do. (*Pauses*) Williamson couldn't be any more than
what he was. And he didn't deliberately set out to do harm
to himself . . . or us. Don't you see that? Oh, I realized
long ago he was a bit different from other boys, but that
didn't matter! Not to me. And he did care about the family
. . . but not like you . . . no one does! (*Silence*) This
family is nothing but ghosts! Especially now. I don't think
any of our family members were so special while they
lived. They look better in retrospect. Well, maybe great-
grandmother Elizabeth was special, but Lord knows,
sometimes I wonder why she wanted to come way off

down here to this wilderness. Maybe she was hiding something. Who knows.

MARGARET: I just see it all as a waste . . . a wasted life. He could have been something special.

MILLER (*in a rage*): He *was* something special. He could have been up there on that stage at Carnegie Hall . . . but he was happiest when he was playing in that dinky little bar in the Village. And he made everybody that came in there feel good about themselves. And that's hard to do today when you see so many of your friends dying . . . and those still alive afraid to reach out. You don't know how rough it is out there when you've got all these people and groups screaming . . . SHAME . . . SHAME . . . ON YOU . . . YOU FAGGOTS! GOD BLESS AIDS. . . . YOU'RE GETTING JUST WHAT YOU DESERVE! (*Miller begins to cough violently. Nora hurriedly gets him some tea from the table*) I'm sorry . . . I shouldn't have gone on like that. Bill didn't deserve AIDS. . . . no one does . . . certainly not Marvin. (*Silence for a moment*) Marvin was my best friend. I thought we would always be together. We were like a team . . . Marvin and Mason . . . and then Bill came along. I almost went out of my mind the way Marvin flipped over him. But I knew all along that our chemistry just wasn't right. We were too much alike. But, with Bill and Marvin . . . well, that match was made in heaven. If I hadn't learned that I would have lost Marvin as a friend. I couldn't do that. He meant too much to me. He was too much a part of my life. And, I couldn't hate Bill. He was just too nice of a guy . . . (*sighs*) he didn't steal Marvin away from me. It just happened. Both of them were something special. (*Silence*) Now, if you will excuse me . . . I think I had best be going . . . I feel a bit tired. This heat is something else. . . .

NORA: Oh, please, don't go . . . stay. We want you to stay . . .

MILLER: It's been a long day and my doctor warned me to not overtax myself . . . he really didn't want me to make this trip, but I had to.

NORA: Oh . . . I'm so glad you did. You'll never know how glad. If all of Bill's friends are like you, then I am most thankful. And grateful. (*Miller takes out the box and hands it to Nora*) Oh! It's so heavy for such a small box . . . I wouldn't have thought that . . . I can't believe this is all that's left . . . this small box. I never did like an open casket . . . but it did say death. But this . . . this could be anything . . . a present even!

MILLER: Oh . . . remember . . . if you decide that you really want to see Waterbury, come to New York and I'll drive you up. That includes you, too, Miss Gravlee. But, be prepared. It's changed hands since 1826, so brush up on your Spanish.

(*Miller leans over and gives Nora a kiss on the cheek*)

NORA: We may just come up! Yes . . . we might do that!

(*Miller nods to Margaret*)

MILLER: Miss Gravlee . . . it was a pleasure. Goodbye . . .

(*Miller picks up his bag, grabs his coat, takes a last look at the room, then leaves. Nora closes the front door and leans on it. Margaret remains seated*)

NORA: I liked him . . . I wish he had spent the evening. (*Nora, still holding the box, hugs it to her breast. Excited;*

has an idea) Well . . . I know one thing. I'm going to make sure that Bill will be happy in his final resting place. It's the least I can do for him now. There's no sense in putting him in the ground up there at that old cemetery with all those Gravlees.

MARGARET: What are you getting at?

NORA: I'm taking these ashes to Montevallo and I'm gonna spread them to the winds all around the farm. Mason said that's where he was happiest and that's where he should be.

MARGARET: That . . . wouldn't be . . . proper! Besides . . . I've already ordered a small marker to go next to his father's . . .

NORA: Go ahead . . . put all the markers you want up there . . . even one that says "Here lies the end of a line . . . the last male Gravlee." But, he won't be there. He'll be all over the farm and half of Shelby County. Oh, he'd like that, I'm sure. (*Pause*) Oh . . . come on, Margaret. Let's start doing things differently from now on. Neither of us has much time left even though grandmother lived to be 102. You know, Margaret . . . we're both going to be dead for a l-o-n-g time . . . you know that, don't you? Well, right now, let's start enjoying what time we have left!

MARGARET: Enjoy ourselves? Have you lost your senses?

NORA: No . . . I've just found them! (*Nora adjusts the fan, takes in breeze*) Maybe we could go up to Connecticut in October when it's cool . . . I'd love to see all those beautiful leaves . . . (*Goes to phone, looks up a number and dials*)

MARGARET: What are you up to, for heaven's sake?

NORA: Hello? Sears? Please give me the appliance section.

MARGARET: Nor. . . . ah!

NORA: Appliances? This is Mrs. Ashton at 1353 Highland Avenue. I want a room air conditioner . . . and I want it installed today! (*Margaret lets out an audible moan*)

NORA: On second thought . . . make that two!

(*End of play.*)

Appendix I

Guidelines for Entering the Competition

Winning scripts are produced in New York by The Open Book under the Actors Equity Showcase Code. Playwrights receive contracts that conform to Dramatists Guild standards. Separate negotiations with *The Fireside Theatre* are conducted in the event of publication.

Scripts may be drama, prose and/or poetry. Entries need not be in readers theatre format, but winning entries may require adaptation or permission to adapt. Entries must not have been professionally produced recently within a one hundred mile radius of New York City.

Adaptations are acceptable if source material is in public domain, or if a copy of a permission license is included, but do not submit scripts that are merely scissors-and-paste versions of the work of others. To vie with the original scripts we receive, adaptations must be as brilliantly inventive as Ted Eiland's **The Most Dangerous Woman.**

Do not submit scripts with elaborate lighting or sets, especially multiple settings, unless effects can be simplified without destroying the work's dramatic effectiveness. If simplifying your set would make your show look like a staged reading, it is wrong for The Open Book. Scripts chosen for production must be cut or rewritten to eliminate onstage smoking. Sound effects and *a cappella* music are acceptable. Scripts should not require copyrighted music unless the playwright is prepared to obtain permission for its use. As for shows that require a piano, we will consider them, but they are less likely to be selected.

Do not submit scripts with casts of more than nine characters and be aware that small casts (from one to six performers) *are very strongly preferred.* Strong women's roles are always welcome. Regretfully, we are not able to perform scripts that demand child actors or onstage animals. In all cases, in keeping with Actors Equity Association policies, as well as readers theatre tradition, we reserve the right to cast nontraditionally.

Maximum playing time of scripts should be no more than two hours *including one intermission*. One-act plays are acceptable.

Scripts must be typed on one side only of white paper. *Include a list of characters immediately after the title page.*

Send one copy of each entry with a handling fee of ten dollars ($10.00) *for each entry* (two or three one-act plays related in plot, character and/or theme are counted as a single entry) by December 1 to The Open Book, 525 West End Avenue, # 12E, New York NY 10024-3207.

Make checks or money orders to "The Open Book." NO CASH! Fees are tax-deductible to the full extent permitted by law. If you wish script(s) returned, enclose a self-addressed stamped envelope large enough for the script(s). If you want to ascertain that your script was received, enclose a self-addressed stamped postcard. Include a biographical sketch. If applicable, enclose production history, reviews, programs.

The competition will be held annually till further notice. But if your copy of this book is more than a few years past 1996, you may wish to query us at the above address. Don't forget to include a self-addressed, stamped envelope for the reply.

An earlier anthology of the winning scripts in the first national readers theatre playwrighting competition *Readers Theatre, What It Is, How to Stage It, and Four Award-Winning Plays* is available for $25.00 plus $4.00 postage and handling from Wildside Press, 522 Park Avenue, Berkeley Heights NJ 07922.

Appendix II

Other Recommended Scripts

The following seven plays reached the semifinal round in the second national readers theatre competition. Some were written for the conventional theatre, but all are easily adaptable to the readers theatre format.

For details concerning the availability of these scripts, write to individual authors c/o **The Open Book, 525 West End Avenue, # 12E, New York NY 10024-3207.**

NOTE: You MUST enclose a stamped envelope with your query or we will not be able to forward it to the playwright.

Diary of the Seducer by Mary Hazzard is an engrossing ironic drama set in nineteenth-century Copenhagen. An idealistic young man conceives a passion for Cordelia, whose name conjures up Shakespeare's tragic heroine, but he is in love with the idea of love and is unprepared for reality. Excellent roles for four women and two men. Play may be simply staged in a unit set with several playing areas. Period costuming is advisable.

Felix and Fanny by Myla Lichtman-Fields provides a fascinating look into the loves and career frustrations of the musician-siblings, Felix and Fanny Mendelssohn. This lively two-person play explores the sexist and anti–Semitic German society of 1821–47 that prevented Fanny Mendelssohn-Hensel from developing concert skills like her illustrious brother Felix, who published many of his sister's compositions under his own name. Performable in a single setting. Period costuming and musical interludes optional, but desirable.

The Passionate Victorian by Charles A. Pulaski provides a dramatic tour de force for one actor who portrays the renowned poet Christina Rossetti from age twenty in 1850 to her demise at sixty-four in 1894. The play explores her life, her poetry and her friendships with fellow poets Swinburne,

Lewis Carroll and her brother Dante Gabriel Rossetti, but the dramatic core of this passionate monodrama is decidedly Rossetti's passionate love affair.

The Robot by Donnally Miller is a one-act play about an inventor who, deprived of the woman he loves, builds a robot to substitute for her. This is no *Twilight Zone* clone, but an odd combination of Lord Dunsany and the theatre of the absurd, with an understated, yet disturbing ending. Three men, one woman.

The Salon of Madame de Stael by Verna Safran is an effective one-woman show about the leading socialite of Napoleonic France, a woman whose vociferous ties to controversial political and literary figures, including Talleyrand and Chateaubriand, eventually led to her expulsion from France by the tyrant she both loved and detested. Relevancy to modern America is apparent from the very beginning of this script about one of history's most truly vivacious women. The set should suggest an early 1800's French drawing room. Period props and costumes would be effective.

Sisters & Brothers, Husbands & Wives by Caroline E. Wood is a rich nonpareil that mingles elements of romantic comedy and gently autumnal drama. Written by the author of *The Immigrant Garden,* which placed third in our first national readers theatre playwrighting competition, the script requires two men, two women and a simple set.

'64 Blue Letters by Constance Alexander is a "living high school year book" of 1964, that watershed year just before times started "a-changing" in America. The Open Book played this script as a first act to the same author's first prize-winning **Kilroy Was Here,** elsewhere in this volume. Three women, two men.

The End of My Rope by Robert Hawkins is a melodrama in one act by the author of *Quiet! Three Ladies Laughing,* which placed fourth in our first national readers theatre playwrighting competition, and **The End of a Line,** included in this volume. Set in a suburban Connecticut kitchen, this eerie, yet amusing play is about a mysterious professional male "nurse-companion" who is more or less of a traveling "sales rep" for Hell. Two men, one woman.